the DOG

trainer's guide to

PARENTING

*Rewarding Good Behavior, Practicing Patience
and Other Positive Techniques That Work*

the DOG trainer's guide to PARENTING

*Rewarding Good Behavior, Practicing Patience
and Other Positive Techniques That Work*

by Harold R. Hansen

SOURCEBOOKS, INC.®
NAPERVILLE, ILLINOIS

Published by Sourcebooks, Inc.
P.O. Box 4410
Naperville, IL 60567-4410
630.961.3900
Fax: 630.961.2168

Library of Congress Cataloging-in-Publication Data
Hansen, Harold R.
    The dog trainer's guide to parenting: rewarding good behavior, practicing
    patience and other positive techniques that work / Harold R. Hansen
        p. cm.
        ISBN 1-57071-510-6 (alk. Paper)
1. Discipline of children. 2. Parenting. I. Title.
    HQ770.4.H36 2000
    649'.64—dc21

                                                                00-024732

Printed and bound in the United States of America
VHG 10 9 8 7 6 5 4 3 2 1

Dedication

Dedicated with my love to
my wife and best friend, Patricia.

Acknowledgments

My profound thanks to:

My family, Heather and Tyler.

My mother, Alfa, a survivor who lost a son
before I was born, and lost her husband a year after
I came along. Thanks for doing your best.

Bob, Carl, and Shirley for being the best
older cousins a kid could ever have.

William (the Line*) Koehler, for his clarity and support.
*Bill was a Lion too, but Line is the nickname.

Britta Putjenter, without whom "Heeling Free"
would never have gone from a dream to a dog school.

Gillian Holloway, for her thoughtful and helpful ideas.

Lee Stone, whose wise words prompted me
to stop talking about writing, and sit down and do it.

Bob Weiss and Barbara Perry Weiss, for their friendship,
sense of humor, and encouragement.

Major, who for twelve years helped me with my classes,
and was my wonderful companion dog. RIP my friend.

All of my students, both the people and dogs,
for all they have taught me.

Table of Contents

Foreword

"You can see a lot if you look."
— Yogi Bear

Is it OK for one friend to disclose another friend's secret? I am going to disclose anyway.

Harold Hansen does not train dogs! Now, it is true that he has run a dog school for a very long time, and that almost all the dog owners in our city have, at some time, had contact with him and his well-known "dog school." But he is not a dog trainer. Nor has he misled people into believing that he is. It's just a simple matter of people seeing what they want to see. It is easier to see the dog as needing the expert advice and the training than it is to confront our own responsibilities (and worse, maybe our inadequacies) in this regard. "So what, or whom, does he train?" I'll tell you in a moment.

For almost forty years, I have been actively involved in academic and clinical psychology: for most of that time I have been a professor of psychology specializing in marital relationships. I take a special interest in observing and evaluating how couples interact. I am concerned with what they do that gets them into trouble and some of the ways that can help them untangle their unfruitful approaches to adult intimacy and satisfaction.

By now, you may be asking yourself, "What do a dog trainer and a marital psychologist have in common when it comes to a book on parenting?" When it comes to behavior, we share an immense interest in how people interact with their families, their kids, and their pets. So much of the time the same laws of nature apply to the interactions of family members, and here I include non-human (but active!) family members. We are fascinated by the similarities in how people's lives are influenced not only by each other, but also by their kids and their pets.

Perhaps it would be more correct to say that Harold Hansen trains people, not dogs. But even here I question the adequacy of the characterization. Harold does not set out to teach specific steps to be taken in a fixed order, much as one would train a person to ride a bicycle. He does provide a set of rules that defines a framework for viewing behavior—a context if you will. When Hansen talks about dogs, he often alludes to what the dog is thinking. Now, I am sure no one knows what (or if!) a dog thinks. Nonetheless, Harold has generated a very useful scheme for viewing the interactions of dog and owner. This context, this way of viewing the behavior of both parties, leads to more enjoyable and more reliable interactions between the two. Further, I believe it is immediately applicable to contacts in the human-to-human realm.

Hansen's expertise offers us avenues that will strengthen the bonds between parents and their children. He has considerable information that will empower parents and their kids, information that will greatly enhance mutual respect and positive regard. Harold used to tell how some people wanted to send their dogs to him to be trained in absentia: the owner didn't wish to get involved. "Just train Fido and send him back to me trained!" (How many times have I heard, "Well look doc, just straighten her out and everything will be fine.") I am reminded of that bit of Buddhist philosophical wisdom that asks, "What is the sound of one hand clapping?"

Throughout this book, Hansen combines, in a charming and humane manner, the observations he has made about himself, his human-pet student pairs, and what approaches have actually produced results. If this is expertise with a capital "E," it sure is easy to swallow! Yet, the entire thrust of this book will enable parents and their kids to utilize their inner resources constructively as they go about the business of getting along with one another. I used to jokingly tell my own children that it was in their best interests that they make me happy. Although that may have been less than politically correct at the time—and worse yet, self-serving—it did reflect an important truism: there are necessary skills when driving on the two-way streets of family life. Harold Hansen offers examples of these skills; the rest is up to us.

Robert L. Weiss, Ph.D.
Eugene, Oregon

Introduction

Does It Work With Kids Too?

Since I opened "Heeling Free" Dog School twenty-three years ago, people have asked me, "Does this approach work with kids too?" Then they laugh a little. A therapist friend of mine says that when people laugh as they make a statement, it usually means the subject is touchy for them. One woman came right out and said, "I wish I could take a class that would help me with my kids as much as your dog class helped me with my dog."

We Already Treat Kids and Dogs the Same

A dog owner called and began telling me about her dog's behavior problem. As she spoke, her dog barked and her child screamed. She said, "Excuse me," and then yelled, "Shut up," at both of them. She came back on the line, but the dog continued barking and the child kept screaming. She did the same thing to quiet the dog and child, and it didn't work with either one.

While this didn't exactly answer the question "Does it work with kids too?" it certainly proved the opposite. If yelling doesn't always work with dogs, it may not always work with kids either.

This call brought to my attention that we might already be treating our dogs and children the same way. We yell at our dogs and we yell at our kids.

Our problem isn't that we are using the same ideas with our dogs and our kids; the problem is that we use similar ideas that don't work with either dogs or kids. Please don't think that I believe that all dog training theories are perfect and should be applied to parenting. Some dog training principles are nonsense and if the ideas don't work with dogs, applying them to parenting is ridiculous.

This Is Not Choke-Chains for Children

Parents who know little about dog training may think of it only as discipline using a choke-chain. Comparing parenting and this choke-chain image of dog training is offensive. Let me assure you this isn't about using a leash and a choke-chain in order to get a child to obey!

When I told one of my friends, who is a psychologist, I was working on a book comparing dog training and parenting he jokingly said, "Oh, no, choke-chains for children," and then added, "Don't you worry about this leading people to abuse their children?" Child abuse is a serious problem, and if I thought for one minute that this book would cause someone to abuse a child, I would not write another word. I believe that at least some child and dog abuse happens because parents and dog owners are frustrated and don't know how to be effective. When they feel they are failing, they resort to abuse. By learning and using the principles of good dog training that I teach in my classes, I hope that parents who read this will not resort to abuse. Obviously, dogs and kids are different, but I believe that the qualities and ideas that make a good dog trainer are similar to those found in a good parent.

Three Reasons to Compare Dog Training to Parenting

1. Seeing It Work with Your Dog Encourages You

If I was a parent who had never trained a dog and someone suggested dog training might help me be a better parent, I would be skeptical. I believe that when you, as a parent, spend a couple of months working with your dog, you see what being consistent does—how rewarding good behavior and correcting harmful behavior is effective. You see how your dog blossoms and becomes confident, and learns that he is competent. You also see that you become more confident as your relationship with your dog improves. When you, as a dog owner, see this happening, you are more likely to spontaneously say, "This might work with my kids, too." I have seen this happen so many times over the last couple of decades with people and their dogs (and with myself) that I am offering the metaphor of dog training because it has worked.

2. Dogs Turn Out Faster Than Kids

The wonderful advantage of testing ideas with dogs first is that you get results in a short time. You can prove that a balance of positive and negative reinforcement is more effective than positive only (which may not work) and negative only (which results in a browbeaten dog). You have heard the expression, "How did your son turn out?" The fact is that dogs-in-training "turn out" a lot faster than children do. You see results in minutes, days, and weeks with a dog. Once you see these results, you are more likely to think of using the principles in parenting.

3. You Can Use Dog Training as Practice For Parenting

While most comparisons I hear deal with dogs and kids misbehaving, one comparison had a positive theme that was very gratifying. A woman called and said, "Harold, I want to thank you." She had taken her Boxer to my dog class three years earlier. I started to say, "I'm glad to hear that your dog is doing well," but she interrupted and said, "Our dog is doing fine, but the real reason I want to thank you is that when my husband and I got married, he didn't want to have kids because he didn't know what kind of a parent he would be. After we took your class, he told me he realized he did have the patience to be a father. Now we have a two-year-old daughter, and I wanted to thank you."

I thought what her husband did was a wonderful idea—using a dog training class and experience with a dog to see if you have the patience to be a good parent.

My Personal Reason—I Did It for My Family

The reason I started comparing dog training and parenting is because of my own family. At fifty-one, I became a stepfather. I had no experience or role models on which to base my actions—I grew up without a father. In fact, we didn't get a television until I was eighteen, and I couldn't even watch the family shows that might have given me some idea about how fathers acted.

As I thought about becoming a parent, I asked myself, "What do you know how to do that will help you?" I turned to dog training. I wrote down some of the ideas that I teach in my dog training class and applied them to parenting. These were not just the ideas like sit and stay (although those words can be useful in parenting as well), but the principles that I teach my dog training students that help them train their dogs. I hope you find some of these ideas will work for you.

Reasons You May Not Like the Comparison

It Won't Work If You Hate Dogs

Comparing dog training and parenting may not appeal to you because your ideas about dogs might be different from mine. If you consider dogs as the lowest creatures on earth, or if you make comments like, "He's a dirty dog," then you don't think much of dogs. It wouldn't make sense to apply your ideas about dogs (and dog training) to children (and parenting) if you don't like dogs.

Instead of thinking that I am asking you to apply a lower set of standards to your child, let me turn this around by asking, "Are you treating your child at least as well as you are treating your dog?"

You May Have Had a Bad Experience with a Dog

If you had a dog that you were not able to train, you will feel uncomfortable with this idea. You may think, "What I did to train my dog didn't work, and there is no way that I want to fail using the same ideas with my kids."

You May Have Taken an Ineffective Training Class

If you took a dog training class that was taught by a poor teacher, or one that didn't produce results, you will not be inclined to use the ideas you learned. Unfortunately, incompetent trainers often can appear successful. When we don't do well in a class, we often wonder if it was our fault, or if the class was not very good. Here are some guidelines to help you tell if either the dog trainer or training method was the problem. Did the trainer keep certain dogs out of class, or kick out the difficult dogs midway through the class? Did any of the dogs make progress? If the instructor couldn't handle the worst dogs in a class, or if none of you (except the Sheltie owners) made progress, it was not your fault.

We Worry about Being Too Pushy

> One of my students was training a dog for an older family member. When she got frustrated, she would cry and ask the dog (who jumped on her and bit her) why he was being so mean. I offered to help and as I took the dog, she said that they were worried about the dog knocking the older person down. She added, "But we don't want him too well-trained." I reassured her that she was in no danger of that happening.

We may not like comparing dog training to parenting because we think, "I don't want to raise children who just obey me, and then become stifled in their creativity and ability." My observation is that most of us don't suffer from having dogs or kids who are too obedient. Our problem is in the opposite direction.

Once, as I got out of my car with my "Heeling Free" Dog School decals on it, a college student approached and said, "So, you are involved in fascist, discipline training for dogs." I smiled, nodded, and walked away. I didn't bother asking him if he thought his mother was a fascist when she taught him to stay out of the street.

There Are Two Kinds of Training

You might have concerns about comparing dog training and parenting because you think dog training is limited to obedience training. There are two major levels of dog training. The first is obedience training. While the word obedience sounds harsh and not very progressive, the reality of life is that people and dogs simply can't run around ignoring the laws of nature and society. As much as I wanted to fly when I was a kid, I learned not to jump off the roof of the four-story apartment house where I grew up. Dogs and kids have to learn they cannot ignore the do-or-die rules, such as, don't cross a street when a car is coming. There are many other rules, including learning to control one's aggression so that we can live together in harmony.

With the second level of training, the dog owner brings out the dog's natural ability. This might be hunting, guarding, pulling a sled, or herding. These dogs need to have some level of obedience training before their natural abilities can be encouraged and refined. Hunting dogs have to learn to work with the hunter rather than running off to hunt on their own. Guard dogs have to learn not to protect you from your seven-year-old daughter. Sled dogs have to learn not to fight with each other. Even the very intelligent and responsive herding dog must learn to take directions from the handler.

Teaching Discipline Allows More Freedom

"I would never 'obedience train' my dog. I want him to be a free spirit."
"Can you let him off-leash?"
"No, he runs away."

We, like the dog owner in this example, may think we are being kind by not teaching our kids discipline. Due to his "kindness," he can never let his dog off-leash to play because his dog will run away. If he does take the risk of letting him off-leash, the dog might get hurt. As parents, we are smart to teach a child discipline, not so we can exercise power, but so that our kids can experience more freedom and independence.

Kids Need Both

Raising a child requires both "obedience training," as well as encouraging the child's individual development. If your child wants to take piano lessons after school and has to take the bus to his lesson, you first have to teach him how to take the bus. He has to learn not to get off the bus where the irresponsible kids hang out, and how to read and use schedules so he will be on time.

Our Parents—Positive or Negative Role Models

When we become parents, we look back at what happened to us as we grew up. We either discipline our kids the way our parents did us, or, if we feel that our parents did not do a great job, we use them as a model for what we do not want to do. I knew what it was like being raised by a loving mom who worried too much. On one embarrassing visit to some relatives when I was ten, she asked if they had a chair she could put next to the bed so I wouldn't fall out. As I grew up, I wasn't sure what being a good parent was all about, but I certainly knew that I did not want to be a parent who worried as much as she did.

Is No Parenting the Opposite of Bad Parenting?

You have probably heard people say, "My parents were too overbearing and no kid of mine is ever going to have to put up with a stupid set of rules like I did." Granted, our parents may not have been the best—in fact some may have been horrible—but we must avoid the trap of thinking the opposite of bad parenting is no parenting.

A woman named Joan goes to the extreme when it comes to the "I am not going to do to my daughter what my parents did to me" philosophy. Joan has two troubled teenagers and says that she fully expects her daughter to be on drugs by the end of the year. When asked what she plans to do to prevent it, she says she won't do anything.

Joan explains that she had a difficult childhood. Her mother was not very strict with her, but she was very critical. The rule was, "I won't set guidelines for you. You can do anything you want, and then I will probably criticize you." Joan's response is, "I'm not going to screw up my child."

In a misdirected effort to protect her daughter from emotional damage, Joan has deliberately not set up rules or structure for her daughter. She changed the rule for her daughter from, "I won't set guidelines for you, you can do anything you want and then I will probably criticize you," to, "I won't set any guidelines for you, you can do anything you want, and I won't say anything to you."

Is this an improvement? Hardly, for now her daughter is faced with another problem. Her mother's failure to establish any structure means that the child has to make it up as she goes along, and if everything she does is acceptable, she has no chance to be recognized for doing something right. Her daughter is angry and unhappy despite (or, because of) the lack of structure. As much as kids are supposed to hate the rules their parents have, I believe if parents don't have any rules for their kids, the kids feel that the parents don't care.

I Wouldn't Have Wanted Myself as My Own Parent

For most of my first thirty-seven years, I walked around with a scowl on my face and a sarcastic word as a response to almost everything. I didn't think I would be a very good parent and decided not to have kids. While I had this image of myself, I didn't realize that it showed until I walked into a camera store to buy a Polaroid camera. After the clerk took my picture, I looked at it and saw myself with my arms folded tightly across my chest and my face looking incredibly angry. I thought, Harold, you are supposed to be here buying a camera, this is fun. You are not waiting for someone to break into your home. Do you always look this angry?

I didn't know what to do with myself, but I stumbled upon a book that helped me realize I could change my personality. As I took steps in that direction, I also noticed that I was becoming more patient with the people who came to my dog training classes. I also found that as I improved my dog training skills, I could be effective without getting angry. I think I equated anger with power. I discovered that knowing how to do things got me much greater results than anger did. It helped me turn an emotional corner.

My experiences with my students, both the people and the dogs, helped me go from that angry, sarcastic sourpuss in the camera shop to who I am today. Now I am happier, more positive, and far more patient.

Making Progress Is More Important Than Perfection

The more I compare dog training and parenting, the stronger I feel about the parallel between being a good dog trainer and being a good parent. I don't present these ideas to you as Moses delivering the Ten Commandments, but as my own story with my particular strengths and weaknesses. My personal life and family life have not been perfect. There were times when I thought, "How can I write a book about parenting if I am not the perfect parent with a perfect family life?" I thought about my dog training career and realized that one reason I got into dog training was because my first dog got killed by a car. Since then, I have lost five dogs to old age. They were seventeen, sixteen, thirteen, ten, and my twelve-year-old dog, Major, who succumbed to cancer while I worked on this book.

As sad as I was about losing them, I did not feel guilty because I had trained them and they had lived a long time. I threw out the idea that I must be perfect to be an expert. I also thought that quitting the book about parenting because things don't always go smoothly, would not go along with my idea that you have to be determined to train a dog, raise a child, or do much of anything else in life.

✔ Dog training can be a helpful metaphor for parenting, and some of the principles that are effective with dogs are equally effective with children.

✔ There are two kinds of training, obedience training and natural ability training.

✔ Discipline leads to more freedom.

✔ Kids need to be taught how to behave and trained to bring out their natural abilities.

Chapter One

What Love Can and Cannot Do

Good parenting begins with love, but love alone may not be enough. You have heard that love can move mountains, but you also know that love alone may not keep your daughter out of a gang, or even get her to clean up her room.

Loving your child is an important part of parenting. Love motivates you, but it may not motivate your child. I see our job as parents as providing love and security, and teaching our children how to grow up. Just loving them, doing everything for them, letting them do whatever they want, and then getting mad at them because they drive us crazy makes no sense at all.

> *"I'm a youth leader for a kid's dog training club. We are having trouble getting our dogs to retrieve. Would you help us?"*
>
> *"I'd be happy to."*
>
> *"Now, we use the Love Method, do you?"*

"What do you mean by the 'Love Method'?"

"We make a happy game of it. We throw the object and then run out and pick it up and show it to the dog to make it fun."

"Does it work?"

"Well, no, the dogs seem happy, but they just watch us pick it up."

"That's not how I do it because it teaches the dog to be happy watching you retrieve."

"But you have to use the Love Method if you are going to help us, because that's what our youth group rules say we have to do."

"I'm not sure how my coming out and doing what isn't working for you already is going to help you."

"You just don't understand." Click.

Some dog training and parenting experts mistakenly assume that love alone will miraculously cure all misbehavior.

I recently watched a television show featuring mothers whose daughters had joined gangs. Near the end of the show, an expert told the moms, "All these girls really need is to know that you love them." One mother jumped up from her chair, burst into tears, and shouted at the expert, "You don't know what you are talking about. I'm tired of people like you blaming me for not loving my daughter. I do love her, but she is in a gang and shoots people. You say that love is the answer, but I've tried love and love doesn't work. What else can I do? You don't know, do you?"

Some people don't love their kids, and it shows. We know that some parents abuse their children, but I am sure they will not be picking up this book to improve their parenting skills. I assume because you are taking the time and effort to read this that you do love your child. I have talked with more than thirty thousand people about their dog behavior problems and I have never once had anyone call and say, "Harold, I need you to help me be more loving and kind."

I Know They Love Me, They Beat Me Up

One of the shocking aspects of teenage gang membership is that some gangs require new members to go through a ritual ceremony in which other gang members beat up the aspiring new member. Society asks, "Why do kids join gangs?" The answer is that the teenager feels loved and accepted by the gang. This explanation really disturbs parents who think, "I love my child and I will do anything for him, and yet he seems to hate me." But if kids join gangs to feel loved and accepted, why do they allow themselves to get beaten up?

This idea doesn't make sense when we apply it to an adult relationship. I doubt that many of us would think, "I met this great new person and we are going out on our first date. I'm going to beat my date up or let my date beat me up as soon as we arrive at the restaurant to show how much we care for each other." If teenagers who join gangs think, "Well, I want to be loved and accepted and so I have to get beaten up to join," that tells us much about their idea of what being accepted means.

Acceptance does have its benefits. For gang members, there certainly must be a feeling of comfort in knowing that if you get killed in a drive-by shooting, your friends will avenge your death; however, being accepted by a gang requires a tremendous commitment to following rules that are a lot stricter than one has to follow while living at home. I can't imagine a parent shooting a child for wearing a red handkerchief instead of a blue one, and I don't think even the most distraught parent would tell a child, "Once you are a member of this family, you are in for life. If you quit this family, we will kill you."

Could it be that teenagers are telling us that rules are important to them? Kids may not like the rules that we have, but I feel we make an error when we think we shouldn't have rules because we fear losing the love of our children. Parents have a job to do—to prepare their kids to be happy, healthy, and productive adults.

As parents, we may catch ourselves thinking we are loving and kind, and yet we discover that our child doesn't know what we expect. Don't make the mistake of blaming the child.

If your child does something wrong that you have never taught him not to do, don't be disappointed. Don't think, "He should have known it wasn't right to do that." Assuming that anyone knows what we want because we love the other person is a trap many of us have fallen into.

Love Alone Won't Teach Him What You Want

A Dachshund owner called and spent ten minutes telling me how much love and kindness she gave her four-year-old dog. She then said, "I can't understand why he still goes to the bathroom on my bed." When I asked her if she ever trained her dog, she said, "No, but…" and then repeated the last ten minutes of how much "love and kindness" she gave the dog.

Love is not a substitute for teaching a dog what he is supposed to know.

Loving your child and teaching your child are two different activities. Love is one of your motivations to teach your child what he needs to know, but just loving your child is not enough.

You may have heard someone say, "I can't understand why he acts so horribly toward me, I love him so much." These words could be spoken by a dog owner, a parent, or an adult in a relationship with another adult. Some of us have the idea that if we love someone enough, that our love will solve everything. Reality proves otherwise. Dogs bite loving owners, children rebel against loving parents, and people abuse others who love them. Obviously, love is not enough.

Love Alone Won't Make Him Do What You Want

> *"Our dog bit our child. I didn't think a dog would bite anyone who loves him."*

The amount of love you have for someone may have little to do with whether they will do what you want, or how they will treat you. Loving someone is no guarantee they will love you back, and even less that they will do what you want them to do. Even if you love your child, your child may still rebel against you.

Love and respect are tied together and go uphill. We love and respect those we look up to rather than look down upon. Imagine loving someone you do not respect. The chances are that you can't imagine it, because you wouldn't do it. The biggest stumbling block keeping us from being better parents is our concern that our children won't love us if we don't allow them to do everything and anything they want.

They'll Still Love You If You Make Them Mind

> *A strong-willed female Rottweiler came to class with her owners. The first week she was the rowdiest dog in class and lunged aggressively at the dogs next to her. I helped her owners get her under control to show them what she could do. After several strong corrections, she straightened out and I was able to balance the corrections with enthusiastic praise.*

The following week a funny thing happened. As I walked around class giving out the instruction sheets to each student, the Rottweiler saw me and ignored her owners. Her little stump of a tail started wagging like crazy and she was happy to see me, even though (or, should I say because) I worked with her. As the class progressed and her owners learned what to do, I was pleased to see that her respect for her owners increased, too.

A parent with a relaxed parenting style and a strong-willed child may worry about imposing rules, and fear that the child will no longer love the parent.

Believing that love alone is all we need has several advantages. It feels good to think that we are kind and loving. Our friends and family think we are wonderful. We have success using love with one child and we optimistically believe that everything will go smoothly with our next child. The following explains why I started using love and then realized that it wasn't always enough.

The Sheltie Syndrome

When I first started training dogs, I had a Shetland Sheepdog named Olaf who was an incredibly smart and cooperative dog. I did so well with him that I imagined I could be a dog trainer, and I opened my own dog training school. If you look at the people who run dog training programs you will see that many of us have, or had, Shetland Sheepdogs, Border Collies, Golden Retrievers, or German Shepherds. These are smart breeds. I think if we started out with a breed that wasn't as easy to train, some of us might have lost our enthusiasm and gone on to do something else.

Having a dog that is very smart, cooperative, and trainable gives you a high level of confidence, but what I found was that the ideas that worked with Olaf didn't always work with the hard-headed, stubborn breeds.

Some dog trainers get stuck when they take training techniques that work well with easy dogs and then apply those ideas to stubborn dogs.

The Sheltie Syndrome involves using dog training techniques that work with the most highly motivated, cooperative, and responsive dogs, and applying the same ideas to the least motivated, most stubborn, and least responsive dogs.

I believe that some experts who write books and appear on television giving advice that all you need to do is love your child, base their theory on the human equivalent of the Sheltie Syndrome. They believe, "Love worked for me when I was a child and it should work for you."

Don't Go on a Guilt Trip with a Love Expert

People who believe in this theory use a system that works with the most highly motivated, cooperative, and responsive kids, and apply the same ideas to the least motivated, most stubborn, and least responsive kids. As parents we may think, "Positive reinforcement worked with my other kids (or with me when I was a child) and I will stick with it even though it is obviously not working with my stubborn child now." When you apply expert ideas to your stubborn child, they may not work and you and your child get blamed, rather than the ineffective ideas.

Results Should Matter More Than Methods

"My dog is biting me, I want to know what your philosophy is and what training methods you use."

"Are you more interested in stopping the biting or in how it is done?"

"I don't want to do anything mean to the dog."
"If you can't solve the problem, what is your next step?"
"Put him to sleep."

Fortunately, we don't put our kids to sleep, but we do run into experts who are more concerned with how things are done rather than whether anything actually happens. Their intentions and methods are more important to them than their results.

There are times when dog owners find it necessary to put a dog down as a last resort to solve a behavior problem. I don't believe it should be the first option and I certainly don't believe it should be done because a person thinks that disciplining the dog is meaner than killing it.

Being An Effective Parent Is Not Mean, Failing to Parent Properly Is Mean

I wrote a letter to one of my students who quit my class because she felt that using a choke-chain on a biting dog was mean.

Your comments about your mother training dogs and never having to use a choke-chain interested me and I hope that you will achieve the same good results with your puppy without having to use a choke-chain.

I am sure that you love your dog, Buddy, or you would not have sought training for him. There are other classes that claim that they use love and kindness and you may be happier with their approach. But, I would beg you for Buddy's sake, be warned that if their love and kindness methods do not work and if the Heeler in Buddy starts coming out in the form of aggressive behavior, the love and kindness folks will probably tell you to put him to sleep.

A woman veterinarian friend of mine and I were discussing a dog she had referred to me. This dog had been to another class and the love and kindness trainer kicked the dog and owner out because it was too aggressive. The owner came to observe one of my classes and felt that I was too strict. The veterinarian said that the owner brought the dog in to have it put to sleep because it was too aggressive. The veterinarian said, "This woman brought this dog in for me to kill it because she thought you were too strict. Funny that these people never accuse me as a veterinarian as being mean even when they want me to destroy their dog."

I sincerely hope that you and Buddy have many wonderful years together and that you can train him using the ideas that are emotionally comfortable to you.

Doing our jobs as parents can be really tough when we have to stand firm and make a child do something he doesn't want to do. Children know that we struggle emotionally between wanting them to love us and having to make them do what we know they should do. Kids can cry and tell us that we don't love them because we don't let them do what they want. The feeling that one of the kids "is mad at me" is hard to accept, but it is part of parenting. If guilt eats away at you when you have to stand firm, think of how you might feel if you don't stand firm and something horrible happens to your child because of your failure to act.

Respect the Differences

We know that each person (adult or child) is an individual. You may be a pleasant, friendly person and your brother or sister may be just the opposite. You had the same parents and you went to the same school, but you are different. We should keep this in mind when we think about our own children. We may feel, "I don't understand it. Three of my kids are easy to get along with, but my fourth one is stubborn as the dickens." We must accept the fact that kids are different. Some kids are very cooperative and easy to work with. All you have to do is explain things once and they understand and will do what is expected for the rest of their lives. With the stubborn child you wake up every morning thinking, "Who is going to win today?"

The Sheltie Syndrome in Schools

Unfortunately, the "It worked for me, it should work for you" theory is applied not only to parenting, but also in the schools our kids attend. While I taught high school, I realized that the rules students follow were developed by teachers and administrators—people who did well enough in college to get a degree that qualified them for their position. When we, as highly motivated educators, design programs that would fit our needs if we were the students, the less motivated students may get lost.

Highly motivated students might make wise selections when offered a number of electives, but others might be confused by too many choices. My high school made it easy for us, limiting the number of electives and guiding each student toward graduation. We selected one of eight areas of interest. Once we made the selection, we simply looked in our handbook. The graduation requirements were in a box that explained how many terms of each subject you had to take. It was simple, you passed all the subjects in the box and you graduated. If you failed to pass one subject, you took it over and passed it, or you didn't graduate.

Another example of assuming all students will act like the most responsible ones is the amount of free time (optimistically called "study time") given to students. A few highly motivated students will go to the library to read about nuclear physics or play the violin, but the lesser motivated students given this free time leave campus, stand around smoking and punching each other, or go into stores to shoplift.

Start With Love, but Don't Stop There

Again, I assume that you approach parenting with love for your child. Imagine that the top of each page of this book says, "Do this with love." Parenting would be easy if love alone worked; unfortunately, it doesn't.

✔ Parental love is very important, but there are some things love alone won't accomplish.

✔ Good parenting begins with love.

✔ Love alone won't teach your children all of what they need to know to be healthy, successful adults.

✔ Love alone won't make your children do what you ask of them.

✔ If you make your child mind, he will still love you.

✔ Don't go on a guilt trip with your children—it doesn't serve them.

✔ Don't let the method matter more than the results.

✔ Start with love, but don't stop there.

Chapter Two

Get Results Without Getting Angry

It was early December and I was shopping at a large store when I saw two parents making exaggerated gestures at a child sitting in the seat of a shopping cart. I was at a distance and at first I thought they were hitting the child. I couldn't hear them saying anything and as I walked toward them I realized that they were yelling at the child in sign language. Apparently, the child had been touching things he wasn't supposed to and the parents were expressing their anger.

If Anger and Yelling Worked, We'd All Be Perfect

One student in my dog class admitted to me, "I can only get my dog to respond when I get angry and yell and I don't want to embarrass myself in front of my family and friends." She asked, "How do I get him to respond without having to get angry?"

If getting angry and yelling at children worked, we would all have well-behaved children. This approach works some of the time, but there are other times when anger and yelling don't work.

Many of us think that we cannot get our child to pay attention to us until, and unless, we get angry. We think that we can't get anything done unless we get angry. When we get to the point of being angry, are we really in control of the situation? No, in fact we get angry because we are frustrated and not in control. Let's find out why anger doesn't always work and what we can do to be more effective without getting angry.

Your Child Knows Your Pattern

The reason a child waits until we get angry before responding is that he knows our pattern. If we asked the child to explain, he would say:

1. *First, you say something in a quiet voice and I ignore you.*

2. *You wait to see what I will do, and when you realize that I am not doing what you want me to, you tell me again.*

3. *I ignore you again.*

4. *When you realize I am ignoring you again, you get angry and yell at me.*

5. *At this point, I know that if I don't respond, you will take some action and make me do what you want.*

Because we each have different patterns, our children may learn to respond differently to each parent. This can be very frustrating when your child only gives you a hard time, but is perfect when the other parent is present. To change your pattern, take action before you get angry.

Don't Blame Others for Your Anger

Don't make the mistake of blaming your child. "He makes me so angry," is about as true as your son explaining a fight at school to you by saying that the other kid's nose ran into your son's fist.

Along with blaming someone else for making us angry we may also say, "Well that's just the way I am, and I cannot control my anger." Some of us blame our ancestry or our parents for our anger.

Your anger is your decision. Anger is a decision we make. If we choose it often enough, it becomes a habit, but it is always a decision we make. The upside is that because it is a decision we make, we don't have to make it.

Imagine being the King or Queen of the world. If everyone (including your children) would do exactly as you commanded, how often would you have to get angry to get what you wanted? The answer is simple. You would never have to get angry because all of your wishes would come true. Your child (and your dog) would behave perfectly.

Better Living Through Anger?

Today, anger seems to be encouraged as a way of getting results. There are books and workshops about anger. We are encouraged to express our anger as a way of dealing with it. I know that many people who have felt oppressed by others are standing up and making things better for themselves and I think it is great. Fortunately, our problems usually have more options than either being a victim and suffering, or getting angry and not doing anything to escape our suffering.

When I talked to a friend about anger, she said, "I'm not going to be a victim anymore." The point is that you don't have to be a victim. Doing something before you get angry, or instead of getting angry, makes you more effective. You get what you want without having to hurt yourself or anyone else. I believe that anger is a gun with two barrels. When I get angry, one barrel is pointing back at me and when I use anger to get what I want, I hurt myself.

If we are having trouble with our kids, we may think anger is our only solution. We may find that if we get angry, we may get a response. This encourages us to use anger to control our children. We want help because we realize if there are only two sides to the coin, neither feels good and, in many cases, anger still doesn't get us the results we want.

The Anger Trap

I grew up in New York City where, for some of us, there seemed to be a lot of reasons to be angry. Dog training was the first thing I did that forced me to lighten up. I realized that the more effective I became at dog training, the less often I found myself getting angry about my dog misbehaving. I wondered if this applied to other parts of my life as well.

I got through my first two years as a dog trainer before one of my students bit me. I learned two valuable lessons.

Max, a large St. Bernard, reared up on his hind legs and bit my right hand. After he stopped biting, and I got a towel wrapped around my hand to stop the bleeding, I picked up something with which to defend myself and told Max, "Down." He did it and I praised him. I was angry about getting bitten, but I was also pleased that I had gained enough emotional control to praise him when he went down. It was the right thing to do.

Threatening him with, "It's a good thing you did it," or continuing to be mad at him for biting would have been easy, but it would have been wrong.

I was pleased because I realized I had made a lot of emotional progress. I came away from the experience with two lessons. The first taught me to deal with a situation immediately, and when it is over don't stay angry, but let it go.

The second lesson took longer to sink in. I got the idea that when something negative happens I don't have to get angry to get results. As I thought about how I reacted to the bite, I wondered if this dog training wisdom would help me in my personal life.

From Anger to Results—Escaping the Anger Trap

Here is how I escaped the anger trap and helped myself replace the idea of getting angry with the better idea of getting results.

First, I listed all of the disadvantages of getting angry. Here are some of the things I came up with:

1. *When I am angry, I am not in control of the situation.*

2. *Getting angry hurts me. My stomach knots up, I clench my teeth, and I get headaches.*

3. *I tend to do stupid things that do not get me the results that I want.*

4. *I look foolish and people around me think I am a jerk.*

5. *My dog probably thinks I am a jerk.*

6. *It takes me longer to do things when I waste time being angry instead of using my time to get the results I want.*

7. *Another problem with getting angry is it doesn't always work.*

8. *When getting angry doesn't work, I get even angrier.*

Some of us think that getting angry gives us energy, which helps us overcome our problems. I began to think of getting angry as stepping on the gas pedal of my car while at the same time letting go of the steering wheel. You do need energy to get things done and anger can give you that energy, but you also need direction. I found that my anger did generate energy, but letting go of the steering wheel (not thinking) did me more harm.

Whenever something happens that prompts me to get angry, I imagine that I am at a fork in the road. I can choose the road to anger, or I can choose another direction. I call this the road to results. I came up with two questions to ask myself when I am at the fork in the road.

1. *"What do I want to happen?"*

2. *"How do I make it happen?"*

Stop Beating Yourself Up

If things are not going our way and we get angry, we either blame others, or ourselves. I began to think of getting angry as a form of beating myself up. Remember that for me, getting angry gives me headaches, a knot in my stomach, and sore teeth. When I looked at it in that light, I asked myself, "When I do something stupid, does it help me to get angry and beat myself up?" Then I asked myself, "When someone else does something stupid, does it help me to get angry and beat myself up?" When I thought of it that way and answered no to both questions, I decided to be easier on myself. I have been amazed to find much less anger in my life.

Do I make mistakes? Sure. Do others do things that I consider stupid? Of course. What has changed is my reaction to things that don't always go my way. Escaping the anger trap took some time and effort, but I am a lot happier now and probably a lot more fun to be around. What I find really amazing is I have done this without compromising either my integrity or effectiveness.

The Why Trap

Many of us get caught in the "Why did this happen to me?" trap. When we only ask why, we are looking back. This can help if we recognize something we did as the cause of our current problem. But we often stay in the past and fail to do something now that will help us solve the current problem.

Concentrate on the Solution

"He goes on my carpet because he hates me. He walks off the linoleum onto my carpet and goes."

When people call and tell me that their dog is doing things to deliberately make them mad, I suggest they concentrate on solving the problem rather than taking it personally.

(Dogs walk from hard surfaces to soft surfaces to go because the ground outside is soft.)

This idea helps me not to take problems (including dog's, kid's, and adult's misbehavior) personally. I suggest we concentrate on solving our problems with our kids rather than wasting time getting angry.

Kid Admits He Has Fun Doing Stupid Things

I recently had a conversation with a parent whose wife was having some problems with their teenage son. He said his son told his mom that the stupid things he did have nothing to do with whether he loves her or not. They were just things he did.

Most of us consider the feelings of those we care about when we do things, but her son didn't. In his own way he was telling her he wasn't doing stupid things to deliberately make her mad. He was doing them because he had fun doing stupid things. We hope he will grow up and realize that what he does has an impact on his family, but until then his words might help us not take a child's misbehavior personally.

The next time you are having problems with your child, instead of wondering why the child is doing this to you personally, use a different approach. Just think that whether it makes you happy or not, your child is doing whatever he wants to please himself. This helps us shift our focus to solving the problem rather than involving our emotions to help us get revenge for deliberate, spiteful behavior. Even if it is spiteful behavior, we will be more effective as parents if we use the two steps to handle the situation:

1. *What do I want to happen?*

2. *How do I make it happen?*

Parenting can be a challenge and it is easy to resort to anger. You can be effective without getting angry and yelling. When you reach the fork in the road, choose the road to results rather than the road to anger.

An even smarter way to do this is to take action before you reach the fork in the road. This involves our next step, which is planning.

✔ Parents can be effective without yelling and getting angry.

✔ If anger and yelling worked, we'd all have perfect kids (and dogs).

✔ Your child ignores you because he knows your pattern.

✔ Whether or not to be angry is your decision.

✔ You can get results without getting angry.

✔ Concentrate on the solution.

Chapter Three

Plan Rather Than React

Many of us plan our days, our work, our vacations, and other areas of life, but when it comes to dog training and parenting we just make it up as we go along. Failing to plan means we have to play catch up, rather than being a step ahead. We have the same problems over and over. When I have a problem arise that I hadn't anticipated, I smile and tell myself, "Harold, that was ignorance." If that same problem arises again because, even though I knew it might happen, I didn't do anything to prevent it, I tell myself, "Harold, that was stupidity."

Make a List

When we cover jumping up in dog class, we set up situations where the dog is on the leash. One is called the "I'm Home" drill. You put your dog on the leash inside your home, then step out the door and close it. With the other end of the leash in your hand you open the door and practice coming home. As you open the door, you say, "Sit," then come in and praise your dog as he sits. If the dog starts jumping up, you can use the leash to make him sit. Some students ask, "What do I do if I come home and my dog jumps when he is off the leash?"

The answer is that your dog wins that round, and you lose. Dog training is usually not a war where you win or lose, but is more like a baseball game with innings. Some innings your dog hits a bunch of home runs and outscores you, but you get the chance to come back and try again.

One smart thing you can do is to sit down with your family and make a list of the things your dog does that you want to change. Once you have your list, set up the situations in advance with your dog on-leash.

By making a list in advance, you can keep one step ahead of your dog.

Like dog training, parenting is usually not a war where there are absolute victories or defeats. It is like baseball where there are innings. If we get outscored by our kids we can think of it as a lesson learned. If we are smart, we will think ahead so that the next time the situation arises, we will be prepared for it.

Have a Plan

When you plan after the fact, there is a good chance your child has already outsmarted you. The reason we get outsmarted is we fail to plan. Planning is wiser than remorse. Make a list of what you have to teach your child. If being safe around traffic is on your list, plan teaching sessions with your child in advance, rather than just reacting when your child gets too near the street. There are rare occasions when something awful happens, either because of an accident, or our failure to anticipate and prepare for a certain danger. While we cannot control everything, we will be miles ahead if we plan, rather than just hope for the best.

Look for patterns and then take action. If your child misbehaves when you go to the supermarket, practice in advance. If you wait until you have to go grocery shopping, you will be torn between getting your shopping done and teaching your child to act reasonably in the supermarket. Knowing that you have to complete your shopping, get home, and cook dinner before your friends arrive creates time pressure. You might decide to endure your child's misbehavior "just this once." Unfortunately, the more success your child has misbehaving, the more likely he is to continue and intensify his efforts. You can pick a time of day when you don't have to rush and take your child to the store. If your child throws a temper tantrum and screams that he wants certain things, calmly and quietly take your child and leave the store. Your child learns you cannot be embarrassed and manipulated by these tantrums. When we don't plan and just react, we don't always come up with the best solutions. If your child outsmarts you, don't get angry. Learn from your experience.

Along with planning, do small, easy things early. That cuts down on the need to do drastic things later.

Don't Confuse Restraining With Training

"We're not going to train our dog. We keep the door closed and we keep her on a leash when we take her out."

While this is smarter than not having a leash on, it overlooks what happens if the dog gets out the door off-leash. Restraining a dog recognizes a potential problem and prevents it from happening. Training assumes the worst will happen and teaches the dog to perform reliably when the leash is off and the door is open.

What does this have to do with parenting? If you walk on the sidewalk holding your child's hand, you are restraining the child from running out in the street. After you train your child to remain safely on the sidewalk, you no longer have to restrain the child.

Prevention and Problem Solving

A second parallel is to understand the difference between prevention and problem solving. Prevention is an important part of planning, but prevention must happen before an incident takes place. Prevention may prevent the problem, but may not solve the problem once it exists.

If we are concerned about a child falling down a flight of stairs at home, we can place a childproof barrier at the top of the stairs until the child learns how to negotiate the stairs. This is a good prevention step. As long as the cover is in place, everything should be fine.

A smarter step is to teach our kids to how to walk up and down the stairs, holding on to the railing so that they will not fall. The advantage of the problem-solving approach (teaching how to walk up and down stairs) is that it will work even if someone forgets to put the barrier up or if your child encounters other stairs that do not have a barrier. With the mechanical prevention approach (the childproof stair barrier), the barrier must be in place and other stairs that do not have a barrier will not be safe for the child.

Be aware of the difference between prevention programs and problem-solving programs. Getting a child involved in scouting might be a good prevention step, but if your child has serious problems, look for more appropriate help.

You should look for parenting information that is appropriate for your child's age and systematically teach your child the skills he needs to survive.

Be sure the prevention step does not teach dangerous behavior. We all know that we should stop when we see a school bus come to a stop, with its red lights flashing. While this no doubt saves children who get out of the school bus, walk in front of the bus, and cross the street, I think this is teaching kids a very dangerous behavior. Basically, it is teaching the child that you can get off of a bus, walk in front of it (and not get run over by the bus), and then cross the street safely. You might think, "Kids can tell the difference between being on a school bus and a regular bus." Most probably can, but I have my doubts when I see drivers stopping behind commuter buses. The driver of that car obviously is not aware that school and commuter buses have different rules associated with them. Might we wonder if that same driver may one day be on a bus and assume that he can get off and walk in front of it because he mistakenly thinks that cars will stop behind the bus? I am certainly not in favor of repealing the law regarding stopping for school buses, but I would like to see children taught not to run out into traffic without first looking.

As a preventative measure, this example does teach dangerous behavior. However, it can be dealt with safely if you explain to your child the reason behind the rule. Learning to know the difference between prevention and problem solving will make a large impact on how you teach and train.

Hope or Plan?

The words plan and hope are not the same. I recently spoke with a family whose dog was growling at their one-year-old son. I suggested they had a dangerous situation and advised them to train the dog. At the end of the conversation, when I asked if they wanted to know when the next dog class started, they said, "We are not sure what we will do. We just hope it won't get any worse."

I wondered how anyone could overlook such obvious danger signals? How would the child feel if he knew his parents were aware of a dangerous situation and didn't plan to take care of it? Would he say, "Yes, our dog is growling at me, but I'll be protected because my parents hope nothing will happen?"

✔ Planning is better than reacting and performing damage control.

✔ Have a plan.

✔ Set things up in advance.

✔ Do small, easy things early.

✔ Don't confuse restraining with training.

✔ Prevention and problem solving can go a long way in raising kids.

✔ Hoping is not the same as planning.

Chapter Four

Neither a Doormat Nor a Dictator

Once we turn our anger into emotional energy that is working for us, rather than against us, we can use two other ideas that will help. As parents, we do a balancing act, looking for the right combination of patience and determination. Some of us are so determined, we lack patience; and some of us are so patient, we lack determination.

Kids Are Not Perfect

"Our puppy still isn't housebroken."
"How old is he?"
"Eight weeks old."
"Well, I don't know about you, but I think I was in diapers until I was about two years old. Perhaps a little patience might help."

As parents, we need a lot of patience, and we should remember that our kids were not born perfect...like we were.

Teaching Requires Patience

Being patient does not mean being a doormat or letting your child do anything he pleases. It means keeping a level head while you are doing something that may not be moving along quite as fast, or as well, as you would like. It means giving your child enough time and help to understand the lessons you are teaching. Kids don't always get things right the first time. Do you remember when you had to learn something difficult? Would you have learned faster if the person teaching you had lost patience with you? When we have trouble learning something, the last thing we need is the additional burden of an impatient teacher.

If your patience runs out and your child isn't learning the lesson you are teaching, the problem may be with the way you are teaching.

Once the child learns the lesson, we have to follow through. This is when we switch from the child knowing what to do, to the child doing it. You may have heard a parent say, "She knows what I want her to do, but she only does it when she wants to." While this is frustrating, it does prove we succeeded in teaching. This job requires patience. Once we finish teaching, and the child knows what to do but doesn't want to do it, then we must shift gears from patience to determination.

Have Realistic Expectations

Here are the top five most interesting training requests people have made for training.

1) I want to send my dog away for training so he will learn to stay home.

2) My neighbor likes my dog, but her husband doesn't. Can I train my dog so that he can play at the neighbor's until the husband comes home at five o'clock?

3) I own a horse boarding stable. My husband and I keep an eye on the stable until 5:00 P.M. and then I want my dog to keep out ONLY the people who have not paid their boarding bill.

4) My dog is making trails in my backyard. Can I train my dog to never walk in the same place twice?

5) I manage a trucking company and need a guard dog that will protect the trucks from everyone, except the drivers.

Remember that your dog is a dog. With that in mind, keep your expectations reasonable.

When I was fourteen years old, we visited a family with a two-year-old boy. I brought a tennis ball along to keep myself amused, and decided to play ball with him. He could bounce the ball to me and I assumed that he could catch just as well. The first time I bounced it to him he made a clapping motion with his hands, but missed the ball and got hit on the chin. He picked the ball up off the ground and bounced it to me again. I bounced it back. He again clapped his hands, got hit on the chin, and started crying. Obviously, he did not yet have the hand/eye coordination to catch the ball. I was expecting him to do something that he was not ready to learn.

Be More Stubborn Than Your Child

"I have a little three-year-old Chihuahua that isn't house-broken yet and I want to put in new carpet, do you have any ideas?"

"How often do you take the dog out?"

"Well, we tried it once."

"You mean you take the dog out only once a day?"

"No, I mean we tried taking him out once. Actually we did it two or three times, but it didn't work."

Don't give up the moment you run into resistance.

Try Not to Try

A parent called about her dog biting their five-year-old son, who was hitting the dog. When I asked if the parents stopped the child from hitting the dog, the parent said, "Well, not yet, but we tried explaining it to him." Whenever someone tells me that they will try or that they are trying to do something, I think of a wedding ceremony. At that all-important moment when the big question is asked, how would you feel if your spouse said, "I'll try," instead of "I do?"

We owe it to the child to explain that if he hits a dog, the dog may bite back, however, explaining is part of teaching, and we not only have to teach, but also make sure that the lesson is followed. An explanation may be enough to get the child to stop hitting the dog, but if it doesn't work, don't quit there.

Another parent called and told me his dog was biting his child. I asked how old his child was and what the child was doing to the dog. He said his son was three years old and teased the dog. When I told him I could help him teach his dog to leave his child alone, but he would have to get his son to stop teasing the dog, he laughed and said, "He's three years old, you can't do anything with him."

Both of these parents lacked the determination to change their kids' misbehavior. The first parent only made a half-hearted effort and the second felt his child was beyond hope. Here is a good test. Take a piece of paper and write your child's name on it and then draw a horizontal line showing how stubborn your child is. Next, write your name under your child's and draw a line showing how determined (stubborn) you are. If your line is longer than your child's, it means you are more determined and can outlast your child. If your line is shorter than your child's, you will have to figure out how to become more stubborn than your child. Even if your line is shorter right now, you can work to extend.

Both parents, along with lacking determination, wanted to do something to the dog instead of the child. This is a trap that many of us fall into. We have such a strong desire to believe we have raised good kids, we overlook our child's misbehavior. Instead, we blame peer groups and drugs for causing our child to misbehave rather than recognizing that our child chooses his actions.

Do Unto Others

A dog in my class kept leaping up and biting his owner's arm. When I took the dog and he tried to bite me, I corrected him and he stopped. I gave the dog back to the man and the dog started biting him again. He said, "I'm afraid of hurting him."

I mentioned that his dog was biting him and wasn't very concerned about hurting his arm, but the man was afraid to stop the dog from biting. He didn't want to be mean to the dog, and his dog sensed his hesitation.

For some of us, this is a difficult emotional issue. One way to help yourself feel more comfortable about being more determined is to "do unto others as they are doing to you."

Remember that you do not have to respond in kind as one fellow with a pit-bull did. He said, "When my dog bites me, I bite him back." If your five-year-old hits you, you do not have to hit him back, but you must be more determined to stop your child from hitting than your child is to continue hitting you.

Understand that there can be a difference between the method of discipline and one's willingness to consistently stand up to a child's deliberate misbehavior. One parent may come home angry and lash out at a child in a very harsh, inappropriate way for doing something minor. We might call the parent, "very strict." However, after the parent overreacts, the parent may feel guilty, and then make up for it by letting the child get away with things. Another parent may respond to the same misbehaving child by using a more sensible approach, and then following through consistently each time the child misbehaves.

Giving in to a child's deliberate misbehavior teaches the child to be a bully. Don't think of yourself as a bully because you consistently and effectively act more determined than your child. As loving parents, that's our job.

A Smart Puppy Owner Starts Early

"My mother-in-law is giving me a hard time about starting my puppy at seven weeks in puppy class. I told her, 'The class is really for me. Once I know what I am doing, both my puppy and I will be a lot happier.' She believes the puppy is too young to retain anything, but I figure the pup is going to be learning whether I know what I am doing or not."

We have a tendency to think that letting a younger child have his way is acceptable because he is just a little kid and we don't want to appear overbearing. Education starts early, whether or not we chose to accept it. Being more determined than your younger child is emotionally harder—although mentally and physically easier—than doing so with your older child. Our emotions undermine our understanding that it is easier to outsmart, and physically manage, a two-year-old than a teenager.

On the other hand, it is emotionally easier—but mentally and physically harder—to be determined with older kids. As they get older, they get smarter and stronger. We have less trouble emotionally because we assume our kids know more and should behave better as they get older. Also, if our power struggle with the older child increases, we fall back to a position of self-defense and find it easier to justify our determination.

It Is Easy to Loosen Up But Hard to Tighten Up

When I student taught high school, one of my fellow student teachers let her students sit in the windows of the classroom. This was against the school's rules, not so much for safety (the school was all on one floor), but because students with free periods would sit out in the common grounds just outside the window. As the Oregon rain gave way to sunny spring days, my friend started having problems with students opening the windows and climbing out to go sit with their friends. I had enforced this rule all along and didn't have any problems with my students in this manner. We talked about what she might do and I mentioned that I had learned that you can always loosen up your rules, but it is a lot harder to tighten them with kids who are used to the loose ones.

Obviously, we can change rules such as "Don't ever go into the street" for a youngster, to "Look both ways before you cross the street" for the older and more responsible child.

We may think that as a child gets older, we can easily tighten the reins if it becomes necessary. The opposite is true. It is always easier to loosen up our parental authority, as our child becomes more responsible, than it is to tighten up as our child gets older and more irresponsible.

If we are wise, we will start early and teach younger children that we as parents are more determined than they are. It is not physically or mentally difficult to deal with a younger child's temper tantrum, but it can be emotionally difficult. If we wait until the child becomes a teenager, we will still have our emotional struggle and will also find the physical and mental struggle much harder.

Have you ever seen a child who was verbally or emotionally abusing a parent, and you watched as the parent just accepted the abuse? Have you ever had a follow-up conversation with the parent and heard, "I wanted to stop him, but I was afraid I might damage him emotionally if I disciplined him (or didn't let him act out his feelings of frustration)." What would you think about a parent who allowed a child to sit in the street in the middle of traffic, and who refused to move the child for fear of breaking the child's spirit? You would think, "If you don't remove your child from the street and take him to safety, your child won't have any spirit left after he gets hit by a car."

Acting Out Resistance Leads to More Resistance

As far as letting kids act out their resistance to us with the hope the child will run out of rebelliousness, remember that an actor who gets up on a stage and acts out a part does not do it to get acting out of his system. He does it to become a better actor. When we let a child rebel to get it out of his system, we are encouraging the child to be more rebellious.

Forgive, but Remember

Change the wise saying, "forgive and forget," to "forgive, but remember." Forgiving is important, but remembering lessons we learn from our experiences also is important. If you tell your son about the dangers of traffic and the importance of crossing the street safely, and he says he understands, yet dashes out into the traffic anyway, you'd be wise to remember the incident. From this experience you know that even when your child says, "I understand," he may not. Remembering this about your son could alert you to the fact that he may not learn things the first time. This does not mean you should tell him, "Bill, I know you have trouble learning things the first time, remember when you ran out in the street?" It means that after you teach your child how to do something, and ask him if he understands, you will not rely on his statement, you will test him to make sure that he understands.

Testing involves setting up the situation you worked on and testing what your child does rather than asking if he understands.

Remember, but Don't Label

> *"I need to bring my puppy to your class."*
> *"What is your pup's name?"*
> *"Poopy."*

Labels can hurt—and can become self-fulfilling prophecies. Some kids live their lives being beaten over the head by one mistake that they made. Their parents call them a name that describes their mistake or deficiency, and never let them live this mistake down. Such a child will temper his expectations of himself to the label he is given.

"Forgive, but remember" does not mean we should keep bringing up a child's mistake to the child. Some parents always talk about their child within the framework of the mistake. It is normal to remember some of the more interesting things our kids do, and mention these to our relatives and friends. The point is not to keep bringing it up to the child.

When I was in elementary school, one girl in our neighborhood, who was prone to crying, told a group of us that her mom told her that she was a mistake. Lacking sex education in school and having been brought up to think that sex was something that married people did, I didn't understand what she meant. I thought mistakes were things you did in school when you spelled a word wrong or forgot the multiplication tables. She lived with two parents whom we kids assumed were her mom and dad. Her mom told her that she was the product of a one-night stand her mom had when she and her husband had separated briefly. What made this really destructive was that the daughter was paying for her mother's own behavior. This girl actually introduced herself as, "Hello, I'm Phyllis and I'm a mistake."

To make things worse, some of the older kids who knew what she was talking about made fun of her.

Be Consistently Effective

Nearly every dog trainer and parenting expert tells people to "be consistent." My observation of people leads me to believe that while some of us confuse our kids by being inconsistent, most of us are very consistent. The important question is whether we are consistently effective or whether we just keep doing what doesn't work, over and over again.

Patience and Determination Are Decisions

Parents need to be both patient while teaching and determined while enforcing the ideas we have taught. Some of us are more skilled in one of these areas and need to develop the other. Gaining more patience and determination does not require anything drastic like a personality transplant. Patience and determination, like anger, are decisions we make.

We can and should expect a child to live within our behavior guidelines, but it is not our child's job to be born with a personality that does not test our patience and determination.

Our job is to use our skills to help our kids grow up. If we don't know how to cook and we become the parent who has to feed the kids, we learn how to cook. If we have to transport our kids, we learn to drive. We should look at our emotional skills in the same way. We can learn to be more patient and more determined, and we also can learn how to balance these two emotions.

By being both more patient and more determined than our children, we also teach them by our example how to reach their goals in life without being steamrollers or doormats.

Remember, both patience and determination are decisions we make. They are free and we can have as much of each as we wish.

✔ There are times to be patient and times to be determined.

✔ Have realistic expectations.

✔ Be more stubborn than your child.

✔ Try not to try.

✔ Be smart, start early.

✔ It is easy to loosen up, but hard to tighten up.

✔ Acting out rebellion leads to more rebellion.

✔ Forgive, but remember.

✔ Remember, but don't label.

✔ Being consistent doesn't mean doing what doesn't work over and over.

✔ Patience and determination are choices you make.

Chapter Five

Common Emotional Traps

Most of us mean well and think we are doing the right thing when we worry. Our children face many dangers and we do our best to protect them. We teach them how to cross the street safely, and not to touch electrical appliances while they are in the bathtub. We teach them to stay away from strangers and we make sure the innocent-looking five-gallon plastic bucket is kept away from small children who might fall into the bucket and drown. The number of dangers our kids face is overwhelming, and it seems normal to worry.

When we worry, we take one of two paths. The first is being concerned and doing something about it, and the second is just getting stuck in the act of worrying. Both of these actions are motivated by a desire to keep our children safe. You may wonder if there is much difference in these two approaches. Does it matter which one we choose? Yes it does, because a parent living in a state of constant worry can have a negative impact on a child. I know because that's how I grew up.

Parents who worry have good intentions, and it's easy to see how this pattern could develop. Two years before I was born, my mother lost a child at birth. Then I came along, and the following year my father died. I was all she had left. This must have been really hard for a woman who only had an eighth-grade education, and I certainly appreciate all of her efforts to raise me. All of the other kids in our neighborhood had families with a mother at home and a father present. Given those experiences, I, too, might have worried a lot about my only remaining family member.

Worrying Impacts Children

As I grew older, I understood her worry, but it left a mark on me. The message I got was that something bad was almost always going to happen, and it seemed every situation was just another opportunity for me to make a mistake. Like every kid, I did make mistakes occasionally, yet I was no more mistake-prone than any of my friends. But the worrying was always there.

Imagine being handed a glass of milk each day and hearing, "Don't drop it!" What happened to me was that by twelve years old, I was a nervous kid who could not walk across a room holding a glass of milk without shaking. By the time I was nineteen, I would buy a cup of coffee and donut, then hold the plate with the donut on top of the coffee cup, sandwiching the donut plate and saucer in my tightly clamped hands so I could walk to a table. At church, I dreaded communion for fear of dropping the little glass with the wine in it in front of everyone.

Interestingly, when I joined the Air Force, my less-than-steady hand was overlooked when they decided I would be a candidate for repairing nuclear weapons. It was only the fact that my father had been born in Norway, which disqualified me from getting a top-secret security clearance and the job. Funny how things work out for the best and the world was saved from the inevitable destruction that would have occurred if I had been required to repair a hydrogen bomb.

One purpose of this chapter is to help you change your worrying into realistic concern. The next step is to take action that will prevent what you are worrying about from happening. I am not suggesting you ignore the dangers your child may face. Just be aware that worrying without taking action does not help you or your child.

Don't Make Worrying Your Hobby

Let's look at what worrying does for us as parents. The first thing it does is it gives us something to do. This may sound ridiculous, but some people enjoy keeping busy by having problems, both real and imaginary. At a dog training seminar, dog trainer Bill Koehler said, "Some people collect stamps, some collect antiques, and some people collect problems. The worse thing you can do for them is to solve their problem, because then they have nothing."

I recently dealt with a very difficult student who spent ten minutes after the first class telling me that my ideas wouldn't work with her dog. The next week, she called me at least three times telling me that it wouldn't work and didn't work with her dog. She began an interesting pattern that I call the "And then…" pattern. People with this pattern just keeping talking about their problems, "And then he tried to attack the dog next door," "And then he ate my rose bush," "And then he chased my sister's kids." On and on the complaints would go. I felt like making a recording that would randomly repeat, "Oh I see," or, "Really?" or, "That sounds terrible." While I am very helpful, I do not like to be the trash can where people feel that they can just call me up and recite their litany of dog behavior problems. As soon as people start doing that, I do what people who love their problems really dislike, I offer to help them.

I now tell my classes that we don't subscribe to the "And then..." syndrome, but instead we do the "When, then" approach. When someone starts talking about the problem, I immediately change it to "When the dog does this, then you do the following." Apparently, this was not what she was looking for and she left the class after the third week. I know that some people find support groups helpful and I wondered what it would be like to have a dog owner's support group for people who want to talk about their problems without worrying about someone offering to help them solve the problem.

Teach Self-reliance

The second reason we get stuck worrying is the satisfaction we get when we help the helpless. We all get a warm feeling when we help a child, another person, a kitten, a puppy, or even a whale. As a teacher, I am really pleased when someone who learns something from me goes on and does it better than I do. Our job as parents is to help our helpless children grow stronger so they are no longer helpless. Some people appear to want the helper/helpless relationship to continue. Helping our children grow up and leave us may be the ultimate difficulty we face, but that is our job.

We know this is going to happen as they get older and we learn to deal with it. It is when they are younger that we must judge when to stop doing things for them that they can do for themselves, so they can develop a sense of self-reliance.

We must search our souls to make sure we are not encouraging helplessness just because we feel good about being the helper.

Children Need Confidence (in Themselves and in You)

Any time your child gets the idea that you are not sure of what you are doing, your child will react to this experience. If your child is confident and senses that you are not, he will take over. If your child is lacking confidence, he will experience the feeling we would have if we hired a guide to help us, and then realized that the guide knew less than we did.

Imagine being talked into going on a white-water adventure by your spouse. You are afraid of water, but you give in because you are told that you will be going with an "expert guide."

As your trip begins, you ask the guide a question and from his answer you realize that he doesn't know anything about the river. Minutes later, as you approach the first set of rapids, you realize he also doesn't know anything about rafting. To make matters worse, the expert guide who doesn't know what he is doing, looks at you and starts shouting, "Now I'm really worried, you are scared, and are going to panic." You would be praying, "Please make the raft touch the shore so that I can get out and save my life."

Here you are scared to death, and your confidence in your guide is falling apart. This is what a child goes through when growing up with a parent who worries all of the time and who then shifts the focus to the fact that the child is frightened.

Feeling Sorry for the Child

Along with worrying, a second thing some of us do is feel sorry for the child. By worrying (and not taking action) we are destroying our child's confidence in us, and by feeling sorry for the child (thinking he can't do anything on his own) we are destroying the child's confidence in himself.

Put yourself in the position of a child faced with a situation that is confusing, stressful, or just plain scary. Which would you appreciate more, someone who watches your helplessness and feels sorry for you, or someone who helps you past your difficulty?

Some children are blessed with parents who do a wonderful job of providing the stable, secure structure they need. Other kids are not as lucky because their parents refuse to help them, and simply want to feel sorry for them. If you were lacking confidence and all you got was the message, "Yes, there certainly is something wrong with you," how would you feel? You'd feel more insecure. How can a child develop confidence when the parent treats him like a basket case?

What children need if they are lacking confidence is not someone treating them as if they were helpless. They need to be guided through activities that allow them to succeed.

Much of our parenting involves giving emotional support. Simply feeling sorry for someone is not providing the best emotional support. If our child falls and scrapes a knee, he needs first aid and assurances that his knee will get better. Our message to our children should always be that they are strong and will survive.

Don't Worry about Changing His Personality

Parenting involves making difficult decisions. These may be minor or major changes, such as taking a child in for professional help, or seeking a treatment program for drug abuse. In families where the mother and father are separated, a decision may have to be made about which parent the child will live with. Some parents hesitate because they worry, "Will it change his personality?" Our major concern should be, "What is best for the child?"

We wrestle with letting our children experience the consequences of their behavior. We want to protect our kids, and at the same time, let them learn from both the positive and negative consequences of their behavior.

Don't Assume They Will Hate Everything

> *"How is your dog heeling?"*
> *"He doesn't like to heel."*
> *"How is he doing with the sit?"*
> *"He doesn't like to sit."*
> *"How is your dog doing with the stand?"*
> *"He doesn't like to stand."*
> *"How is your dog doing with the stay?"*
> *"He doesn't like to stay."*
> *"How is your dog doing with the down?"*
> *"He doesn't like to go down."*
> *"That's interesting, I've never heard of a dog that hated everything."*

Some of us feel we should not expose our kids to new experiences because they might not like them. Don't worry about them not liking something before they do it.

The benefit in having your kids do things that might not seem fun at first, is that it can turn out to be better than you (or they) might imagine. While I was in the Air Force, I was assigned to go to Greenland for a year. While at first I hated the idea, it turned out to be one of the most interesting experiences of my life.

Not all new experiences work out, and it is wise to take appropriate measures, as my aunt did when she first served me liver at the age of three. I remember sitting at the dinner table and seeing my aunt holding a pail next to me. I asked what it was for and then took my first bite of liver. I quickly discovered why she had the pail handy. At the end of the meal she added, "I wasn't sure if you would like it, but I wanted you to try it." Fortunately, she didn't stop introducing me to other new foods, some of which looked worse (but tasted better) than liver.

One of our jobs as parents is to introduce our children to new experiences. Not all work out, but we shouldn't stop doing new things just because one experience wasn't perfect.

Kids Get Attention by Complaining

One couple complained that their dog would not walk on a leash. I took the dog and started walking. The dog (being hooked to a leash held by someone who was moving) started walking.

Even as the dog walked away with me, the man said, "She just will not walk on the leash." I looked back and said, "But, she is walking on the leash," to which he replied, "Yes, but she will not do it."

Even faced with evidence that their dog was walking on the leash, this couple did not want to let go of their problem.

The fact is that both adults and children get a lot of positive reinforcement when they complain about their problems.

One friend's sixteen-year-old daughter had perfected this technique for getting attention. While the mother was in my office talking about her dog problem, her younger daughter came running in and announced, "Wendy is crying and complaining because she hurt herself." Her mother asked, "What happened?" and was told, "She fell out of the car." As the mother ran out to the car to console Wendy, I wondered how a teenager could fall out of a parked car with the doors closed.

Kick the Complaining Habit

Not only do kids get attention because they complain, parents do, too. As I grew up, worrying and complaining were part of my family life. I did a lot of both until I underwent a conversion. Just as ex-smokers seem more concerned about others smoking, when I stopped complaining, I began to notice it more in others.

I overheard a conversation at an all-you-can-eat buffet restaurant between a parent (who filled her plate until the food was overflowing onto the tray) and her adult son. As they approached the cashier at the end of the serving line, the parent complained, "They give you too much food here, how am I going to eat it all?" When her son reminded her, "But ma, you filled your own plate," she replied, "Yes, but they still give you too much."

I concluded that some people don't know there are options other than complaining. A friend of mine told me that when she moved out on her own she bought a new sofa. Her parents came to visit and she proudly showed her new sofa to them. Her parents began to criticize it, telling her that they don't make things like they used to. She said, "I invite you over to show you my new sofa and all you do is criticize it." Her father looked at her with a genuinely puzzled look and said, "Well, what do you want us to do, be quiet?" Interesting that her parents thought you either complained or kept quiet.

One hot summer day, after I had moved from New York to Oregon, I took my mother shopping and she complained about the weather. She looked at me and complained, "I notice that you don't complain as much as you used to, what's wrong with you?"

If you are a parent who lives in a state of perpetual worry and who complains all of the time, your child will think that everything will always be a problem for you.

Some parents feel comfortable complaining about all of their health, money, and personal problems in front of their kids. As much as my mother complained about many things, she never burdened me with her personal problems. I wonder how a child might feel if burdened with his parent's financial, personal, and marital problems. I believe it is better to deal with our own problems rather than place those burdens on our kids.

Instead of complaining, we can explain to kids that we may have to make some changes to deal with a specific problem. This teaches the child the lesson that when problems come up in life, we look for solutions, rather than just complain about them.

Not everything goes as well as we would like, but we don't want to put a child into a position where he feels like no matter what he does, you will find something to complain about. I remember my mother's last words before she died, "You're a good kid, sometimes you're too good." After she died, I thought about my memories of her worrying, complaining, and feeling sorry for me, I knew that she'd done the best she could, and that those were her ways of showing me that she cared about me. I didn't enjoy it as a kid, but I outgrew it; now I wonder, with a smile, what she would tell me if she could contact me from heaven. I imagine she would say, "Be careful when you get here, these streets of gold are so slippery and that incessant harp music is driving me looney!"

✔ Avoid the most common emotional traps that well-meaning parents encounter.

✔ Worrying harms children.

✔ Turn worry into action.

✔ Don't make worrying your hobby.

✔ Teach self-reliance instead of encouraging helplessness.

✔ Your child needs confidence in himself and you.

✔ Feeling sorry for the child doesn't help the child grow.

✔ Don't worry about changing your child's personality.

✔ Life isn't all spinach and liver; don't assume kids will hate everything.

✔ Sometimes children (and adults) seek attention by complaining.

✔ Kick the complaining habit.

Chapter Six

Building Confidence

L et's look at some of the things that we do with dogs and children who lack confidence. We will see that while we may mean well, we may actually be creating the problem or making it worse.

Working With Dogs That Lack Confidence

The key issue here is that some people think shy dogs or dogs lacking in confidence need consoling and should be treated as disadvantaged. The fact is, simply feeling sorry for the dog and commiserating with the dog encourages the dog to lack confidence.

Apprehension, fear, or anxiety can be either fear of the known or fear of the unknown. If it is fear of the known, you must take steps to stop bad things from happening to the dog. If someone is being abusive to the dog, you should stop that behavior. If the cause of the fear is unknown, you need to replace that fear with structured exercises that your dog will learn and do.

The sit-stay and down-stay exercises are the best structured activities that help dogs gain confidence. As soon as you have solid stays, you will want to start doing stays out-of-sight. This is most easily done by placing a dog on a sit-stay near a corner and then disappearing around the corner. I wait until the dog will do a one minute sit-stay out in front of me and then I start doing very short sit-stays around the corner—starting with only five seconds and then gradually building time up. Once I reach three minutes around the corner with the sit-stay, I replace it with the down-stay, building the time until I reach thirty minutes.

Like children, dogs can pick up clues as to when you are about to leave. You also need to make the times you leave your home as uneventful for your dog as possible. Do not talk to, pick up, or pet your dog as your leave. When you do return home, give your dog some things to do like sit, lie down, come when called. This gets your dog working for praise and attention rather than getting it as we wish to give it.

Separation Anxiety

We are bombarded by television commercials offering drugs that solve many of our medical problems. I feel a little strange going in and telling my doctor that I saw a television commercial about a medicine and I wonder if I might need it. I like to think that my doctor knows about the new medicines and that when I go in for a checkup, he will suggest the medicines I might need. Rather than think, "There is a solution, I might have a problem," I prefer the idea, "I have a problem, is there a solution?"

Now that a medicine is available for "Separation Anxiety" in dogs, we see commercials offering a solution to this problem. No longer do dogs merely chew and destroy our homes, now they suffer from separation anxiety. Ever since dogs were allowed in homes, they have missed their owners, chewed things up, and created messes. I have been through this with one of my dogs, gotten him trained, and have helped many other dog owners with this annoying problem.

Inherited Confidence

Some dogs have to be very pushy to perform their job and because of their breeding are more confident. For other breeds, a high degree of confidence is not required and breeders do not look for that quality when they select dogs for breeding. Other breeds were selectively bred to work cooperatively with other dogs to do a special task and members of that breed are much happier when they have company.

The difference between people breeding dogs and people having children is that while dogs are bred to conform to certain breed standards, we as people usually do not select a mate based on his ability to pull a sled or her ability to herd sheep.

We as people meet someone, fall in love, marry, and have children. They say that opposites attract, but we know that some people with a certain interest and talent (like music) may marry and increase their child's chance of inheriting musical talent.

The result? Children are born with different traits. While some children are born with more confidence, others are born with less. We cannot do anything about this but recognize that children are indeed different and we should not expect all children to accomplish the same things or to have the same levels of confidence. One child may have a talent for drawing while a sibling may be great at doing math problems.

The best way to view this is to think of each child having a range and to help the child move up as high as possible within his range.

Learned Confidence

Along with the genetic factors, a dog's ability to handle stress also is influenced by what the dog experiences and how we teach the dog to deal with potentially stressful situations. The same is true of our children.

Dogs chew, get into our belongings, knock things down, and misbehave when we are not there. (Of course, some dogs do these things even when we are at home.) Part of this may have to do with the fact that when we are home, we keep our dogs entertained. We might make the mistake of playing a lot of games with our dogs that teach our dogs to relate to us orally. We play tug-of-war and when we leave, our dog misses us, finds things with our scent on them and chews them up. Failing to teach our dog to behave by himself while we are home makes it harder for the dog to behave while we are gone.

While playing with our children is an important part of parenting, we also should help them learn how to entertain themselves rather than relying on us to entertain them. In order to teach this, parents should encourage children to entertain themselves, even while an adult is at home. Teaching children self-sufficiency and confidence can be hard for us as parents—we love our children and want to spend time with them. We have lots of fun entertaining our children and we feel good about being their center of attention.

Weaning them from depending on us may at first seem troublesome because a child may pressure us to keep him entertained. We do not have to take a harsh "do or die" approach such as putting a child in water over his head and then expecting him to "sink or swim." Instead, we would teach the child how to move his arms and legs, while supporting him in the water until he develops his skills. Boosting a child's confidence and teaching him to feel comfortable and safe, even while we are not in the room, also needs to be approached step-by-step.

Build your child's confidence before the child faces difficult situations.

Confidence building must take place when your child feels safe. Once your child has gained the confidence he needs to handle the situation, then you can test the child.

A dog owner was referred to me by his veterinarian for help with a behavior problem. The dog had two problems. The first was that the dog was afraid of rain on the roof and the second problem was that the dog lived in Newport, Oregon, which gets over ninety inches of rain each year. I asked if the dog was trained and the dog owner told me that the dog knew how to heel, sit, and stay. (By now, I know that when people tell me that their dog is having a problem but the dog is trained, it isn't.) I told the man that the next time the dog starts to panic, make the dog do something he knows how to do over and over again. By repeating the exercises the dog knows, the dog's fear is lessened.

The next day, the man called back and said, "It didn't work." I asked what happened and he said, "She wouldn't do it." When I reminded him that his dog supposedly knew how to heel, sit, and stay, he said, "Yes, but she wouldn't do it."

I know that this works because one of my dogs was afraid of diesel trucks when I first got him. I taught him how to do the heel, sit, and stay and then had him do those things near diesel trucks. Soon, his fear of diesel trucks disappeared and he could walk past them without a problem.

Preparing your child to deal with confidence issues such as being afraid of water works the same way. You teach the child how to swim and you do it before the child needs the skill. If your child accidentally falls into a pool and doesn't know how to swim, you rescue your child. You don't try to teach the child to swim while he is drowning. You teach your child the skills when the child is safe and comfortable.

Teach your child the skills he needs before he needs them.

Unknowingly Undermining a Child's Confidence

Parents can create anxiety, above and beyond the child's individual response to being left alone, or with another adult. We may actually encourage our child to miss us when we leave. This can happen when we use a tone of voice giving the idea that something unpleasant is happening.

Our anxious, sympathetic tone prompts an anxious response. If our child sees us heading for the door and starts to look sad and act a little unsure, we might think that we are reassuring that everything will be fine, but what we are really doing is setting the stage for and then rewarding anxious behavior.

We make statements such as, "Aren't you going to miss Mommy?" "Daddy hopes you will be all right while he is away." "Aunt Jane won't hurt you." While these statements show the parents care, they are not likely to reassure the child that everything will be fine.

The first statement plants the seed in the child's mind that the child "should" miss Mommy. The second implies that, "The reason Daddy hopes you will be all right is that he has some doubts about what is going to happen to you while he is gone." The third statement just plain scares the heck out of the child. It is like the doctor telling the child that the injection "won't hurt." After a while, the child realizes that when people say this type of thing, it usually does hurt. The child also learns that when a parent offers the child something yummy like ice cream, the parent never says, "Try some ice cream, it won't hurt."

It is perfectly normal to develop this style of thinking. Our parents may have brought us up to the beat of this drummer. If our parents didn't, much, if not most of the "news" we are exposed to paints a picture of at best uncertainty and at worst doom and gloom. For example, each afternoon before the evening news, one of our local television newscasters comes on with a preview of one of the leading stories. "Do you know that the germs on your toothbrush can kill you?" Or, "Heading out for the weekend? The state police will be out in force." "If you think you have it bad, you will meet a family that was wiped out by a fire." Realizing the force of negativity in the news can help you monitor your own spin when talking to your children.

The Danger of Commiserating at the Wrong Time

Expressing sympathy for a child who has experienced a loss or some other misfortune is part of the loving support that we parents provide. What causes problems for the child is our feeling sorry for the child when nothing is wrong. A child may react by thinking that something must be wrong and that the child is indeed a victim.

✔ **Don't mistakenly encourage fearful behavior.**

✔ **Recognize differences in naturally inherited confidence.**

✔ **Encouraging self-reliance helps prevent separation anxiety.**

✔ **Build confidence before it is needed.**

Chapter Seven

A Parent's Most Important Role

Our most important role as parents is to lovingly provide guid-ance and structure because our children don't know about the world. When we raise a child, we have these emotional concerns:

> *"Should I make up guidelines?"*
> *"What should they be?"*
> *"How tough should these guidelines be?"*
> *"How do I teach these guidelines?"*
> *"How do I enforce them?"*
> *"Should I be strict or lenient?"*
> *"Will I damage him emotionally if I provide too much structure or too little?"*

We have an obligation to protect our children by teaching them to be safe. We also have the obligation to teach them to fit into society.

Not every family has the same rules, but one of the kindest things that we can do for our children is to provide a consistent, stable structure for them.

Without Structure, Our Kids Are Not Free, They Are Lost

Imagine a mother polar bear having a cub and thinking, "Who am I to tell my cub what to do? I will let him grow up naturally. I won't teach him to hunt so that he can feed himself, or how to swim so that he doesn't drown. I don't want to inhibit his growth by imposing my ideas on him." Would we think of her as a kind, sensitive parent? Or would we think that if she doesn't teach her cub what he needs to know, there will be one less polar bear on this earth?

How would you feel if you lived in a place where you seemed to be able to do anything you wanted to do? It might seem wonderful, until you were arrested and told you were going to be executed for breaking the law. You would protest that you didn't know that there were laws, and you didn't know that you were breaking the law.

Isn't this what happens to some children? They are allowed to experience total freedom until they overstep a line they may not even know exists. Then, they suffer the consequences.

A friend of mine got divorced and was awarded custody of his kids. He wondered what he was going to do. He decided to take a psychology class to help himself be a better parent. He told me he learned how important consistency is to kids. He learned that you can be strict or lenient or whatever, as long as you are consistent. He called it "being extremely consistent." If there is consistency, our children are relieved of the anxiety of wondering, "What is going to happen next? Do I have to figure out the adult world, or is the adult world going to maintain?" Our children need the certainty of knowing that the way things are now will be the way they are going to be tomorrow, and if they know that, then our children don't have to figure it out. They can say, "I can just trust my parents, and be a kid."

There Are No Rules, Just Good or Bad Moods

"My dog gets up on the sofa and there are times when I don't want him up there."
"So you do let him get on the sofa?"
"Yes."
"How does he know when he should and when he shouldn't be there?"
"I don't know, but there are times when I don't want him up there."

A basic problem with dysfunctional families is that if there are any rules, they can change. The child learns that the rule is whatever pleases the parent at any given time.

The ground is always shifting under the kid's feet. The child learns that any action is OK provided you don't get caught. That is how chronic lying, criminal tendencies, and other dysfunctional behaviors develop. There is no right or wrong, there is only incurring displeasure from authority at random. So if the parent is tired one day and the kid does something he has gotten away with many times before, the child can get punished for it because the parent is in a bad mood, not because a rule exists and is broken.

Don't Bend the Rules, Apply Them or Change Them

You may have heard the expression "Everything counts." I believe "Everything that matters counts." As a parent, I have certain rules that I feel must be followed, but there are some things children can be allowed to decide on their own. If a child wants to keep his room a certain way that is within your range of limits, I see nothing wrong with that. You don't have to have rules for everything, but if you do have rules, observe them. If your child is taught never to open the door at home when a stranger is there, that rule is always enforced. If you allow your child freedom in other areas, that freedom should apply until you are forced to change the rule. To sum it up, your rules should be set and enforced consistently. Don't bend the rules. If the rules aren't working, change them and then apply them consistently. Letting your child get away with a lot of small things, or not expecting your child to be responsible for anything are sure ways to continue having your child do the one thing that really does bother you.

Both Parents Should Agree on, and Enforce the Rules

"My dog jumps on our kids and when I go to stop him, he runs to my husband because he knows my husband won't make him mind."

Everyone involved should be aware of the family rules and be consistent in following through.

I went to a party one evening and watched a group of twelve- to fourteen-year-old children who wanted to get away from the adults and go outside. They went to one parent and asked if they could go out and she said, "No." Minutes later in another room, they asked another parent and he said, "No." They didn't give up and finally found a third parent who said, "Yes." When they came back inside, one of the first two parents asked why they went outside after being told not to, they said, "Well, Mrs. Smith said we could." This not only undermines the parent's instructions, it subtly teaches kids to weasel around a rule rather than respect it.

A Stepparent's Role

After my wife and I married, there were her two children, four dogs and three cats. I jokingly referred to my wife's dogs and cats as my "stepdogs" and "stepcats."

Combining families of dogs, children, and adults can be interesting, frustrating, and challenging. All involved can get along, or some may have difficulty accepting the new situation. We mistakenly think that because two people meet, fall in love, and get married that their children, dogs, and cats also will love each other.

There are so many variables here that I think the only advice that I have is to be sure that both parents sit down and come up with a plan, rather than just coasting along and dealing with problems as they come up.

One parent may want the other to lead, follow, or be equal in parenting and then as things happen, may change and the two have to renegotiate.

My reason for writing this book was to help myself figure out how I should act as a stepparent. My closest similar experience was working as a substitute teacher in junior and senior high school before I got my full-time teaching position. Both as a substitute teacher and a stepparent, I found myself walking into situations that I had not created. I did my best to figure out what was going on and continue doing what I thought should have been done. Even when we think we understand what is expected of us, there are times when things backfire.

The most ridiculous experience I had as a substitute teacher involved following the absent teacher's written instructions. "Show this twenty-minute film and then release the students. They can go to the library to study." The last class was a two-hour class and the students came in, I turned the film on and released them twenty minutes later. I went to the school's office to check out and was called into the vice-principal's office. He told me that I couldn't check out or leave until 3 P.M. and that I was still responsible for the students. He ordered me to go back to the room and stay there until school was over. Fortunately, I had brought a book with me. When I got to the locked classroom, I realized I didn't have a key and just sat down in the hall and read. Being an adult sitting in front of a locked classroom door, I looked rather foolish and several students came by and asked what I was doing. I explained and they laughed.

Being a stepparent can be the same. You think you understand what your spouse wants you to do, you do it, and then realize that you didn't meet your spouse's expectations. Possibly you misunderstood the expectations or perhaps as the situation unfolded, the expectations changed and you were not aware of the changes.

One radio expert says that as a stepparent you have no right to be anything other than a friend to your stepchildren. I find it hard to accept that when it means that one has to live in a state of chaos. I believe that it is fine for the birth and stepparent and the children to decide which rules should govern those living in the home.

When I first met my wife, her Cocker Spaniel was play biting her children and me. I would find it ridiculous to ignore the dog's behavior problem. I stopped him from biting me and he has never bitten the kids or anyone since then. My wife was a little surprised that I corrected him, but was happy that he stopped biting her children.

I can understand that a child may feel it unfair if a stepparent overrides a birth parent's rule or if the stepparent just makes up rules, or is abusive. I also believe that a stepchild will feel more secure in a home where his birth and stepparent agree with and maintain a unified family structure. Some kids may have the attitude, "You are not my parent, you can't make me do anything," toward a stepparent. I will give you ten-to-one odds that the same child will have just as little regard for his birth parent's wishes.

The Difference Between Choices and Requirements

Some of us like our dog to jump up on us, and others don't. You can have your cake and eat it too with this approach. I taught my dog, Major, that when I say, "Let's dance," he can jump up if he wants to. Major has a choice. He doesn't have to jump up but he can. He will only jump up when he hears "Let's dance," and since no one else in my family wants him to jump up, they don't say those words.

On the other hand, when I say, "Come," I expect him to respond every time. That is a requirement.

As parents, we decide our child's choices and requirements. Many activities can be set up as choices, others must be requirements.

We are told, "Give your child choices." Joan, the parent I mentioned who accepted the fact that her daughter would be taking drugs, took this advice to an absurd extreme. She proudly said that her son (who was already taking drugs at fourteen) was at least making his own choices. When asked what she meant, she said he could choose the drugs that he takes. She is actually proud and thinks she is a good parent because she lets her son make choices, "Should I smoke a joint, or take LSD today?"

While giving children choices sounds like a good idea, we should consider whether the child has enough experience to make the best choice. In school, bright kids may select challenging classes, or choose easy classes that allow them to be lazy. Children with less ability may not know what to do. Parenting involves giving children some choices (as long as they are sensible) and allowing them to have experiences which can help teach them to make good decisions.

Give them things to do so they can have new experiences and enjoy the feeling of being part of something. Imagine being incredibly wealthy. What would you do? You might quit your job and buy a bunch of things, but chances are that after a while you would get bored sitting around playing with the toys you bought. You would probably get involved in doing something purposeful.

There are two kinds of choices. The "either/or" choice and the "if/then" choice. An example of the "either/or" choice is telling your child, "You can either go roller skating or swimming." An "if/then" choice is, "If you do your homework before I get home from work, then I will take you out driving for an hour."

Giving Choices Does Not Mean Kids Are Adults

Children should have all of our love, but not everything they want. While we can give our children choices, we cannot have a democracy with our young children. We can pretend that things are equal, but they are not. We may fall prey to the idea that the wishes of children (even if unreasonable and dangerous) are as important as the wishes of those of us who are responsible for them. We have to set up rules and guidelines for our kids. We might feel a little funny doing this because we worry about the impact of our rules on our children. I doubt that any rule you as a parent might make up will have consequences that are as deadly to your child as your failure to set rules.

Kids Don't Fear Requirements As Much As We Imagine

When I taught high school, I was hired to work with students who needed help with basic math in their shop classes. Our school had excellent shop classes, and the students loved them. I thought the school could use the shop classes as a motivator for the kids who were not very good at math. To get into the shop classes they would first have to take a class that would teach basic math. Little did I know that the dreaded "R" (requirement) word had been all but banished or watered down—so much so that the reading requirement for graduating from high school was to read at the eighth-grade level.

One administrator was against my idea. He thought the students would drop out of school rather than take a required math class that would prepare them for taking shop classes. Here was a perfect chance to use a positive motivator (the shop classes) to help students learn the math they needed. By overlooking this opportunity to prepare the students for doing the math in the shop classes, the school put them in the position of failing. What they thought would be their favorite class turned out to be another class they didn't do well in because they couldn't do math. I asked one of the students, "Would you take a required math class if you needed it to take the shop classes you like?" He replied, "I guess so." He had a hard time with math but he didn't say, "If I have to take a math class I am going to give up and quit school." Most kids make an effort to live up to our expectations, particularly if we structure it so that it helps them get what they want.

Don't Lower the Standard, Raise the Child

"Do you have special classes for abused dogs?"

"Your dog can attend a regular class."

"Oh no, you don't understand. He was abused and could never be in with all of the other dogs."

"I had a dog that was lacking confidence and the smartest thing I did with him was train him in a regular class."

"Well my dog is different and he needs a special class."

When parents have this attitude, it can be a combination of a parent wanting the best for the child and at the same time, a desire to make life easier for the child. One major difference between training a dog and parenting a child is that our job of parenting is to prepare the child to grow up and leave. Some children do have special needs, but we should not attempt to protect children from reality. If we lack confidence in our children, we teach them that they are inadequate.

Some school officials and parents are afraid of requiring kids to do things because they fear that the children will be overwhelmed by the requirement and suffer from low self-esteem. I believe the opposite is true. What can elevate our self-esteem more than accomplishing something?

The whole idea of making school and life easier for kids because we think they might be unhappy is ridiculous. If children are required to do something and they make little or no effort and then fail, they will survive. Our job as parents is not to shield our kids from life, nor to make life easier, but to teach them how to survive and succeed.

How Do You Know What to Do?

The good old days were not always as good as today, but I believe that one of the advantages my friends and I had growing up in the 40s and 50s was that most of the people who had an influence on us held similar beliefs. Our parents, teachers, school administrators, the police and criminal justice system, our religious leaders, and neighbors seemed to have a sense of what, at that time, was universally accepted as right and wrong.

This made it easier for our parents to help us grow up because they had a set of rules to teach us rather than having to make them up on their own. Another advantage was that because the community appeared to back up our parents, we were not as likely drift away from the norm.

There were some minor differences, such as whether you could play cards on Sunday, or eat meat on Friday, or dance, but in general there seemed to be a commonly held set of rules. This doesn't mean that everyone was perfect and the rules were never broken. It meant that if the rules were broken we knew that we had done something wrong and that it was our fault.

We have lost that today and it makes our job as parents harder. What do you tell your child when you catch him lying and he responds, "But I wasn't under oath?"

How do you teach your child respect when television programs and music encourage killing police, treating women as dirt, or using drugs?

One of my stepdaughter's friends is Mormon. While many students have religious beliefs, she is picked on by other kids at her high school because of her religion, and what it allows and does not allow her to do. This makes her life a little harder than some of her friends, but she also has the tremendous advantage of always knowing what is right and what is wrong. This helps her when she is faced with decisions that some kids might evaluate on the basis of peer-group pressure and popularity. In her world, being popular is important, but not at the expense of her religious beliefs.

A friend of mine who was a single mom told me she felt her one mistake in raising her child was not to have been involved in an organized religion. She said it was hard making decisions about what to teach as right and wrong because she didn't have a sense of it on her own. She admitted, "I just made it up as I went along."

Some families who are not involved in religion can manage quite well if the parents have a set of values they can pass on to their children. If we don't have a religious background to help us formulate our rules, and we haven't thought out our values, it will be hard to pass along to our children what we don't have.

Don't be afraid to teach your child your values. If you feel, "I will let my child decide for himself," the chances are that your child will not create a set of values on his own, but will simply listen to others who are more than willing to share their values with him.

Our values, our knowledge of the world, and the way we live our lives, are part of the structure we provide for our children. As much as children bounce off the limits we set for them, they still need the limits.

A television show featured several families where the parents had allowed the kids to take over the leadership of the family. I saw a two-year-old saying terrible things to his parents. His parents just seemed to overlook the behavior or make excuses for it. There was a moment after this little boy screamed his demands at his parents, when he stopped just for a fraction of a second. At that moment his expression changed briefly. It went from a look of power to a look of confusion and surprise that sent the message, "I am only two years old. You are my parents, why are you letting me get away with this?" and then he continued his tantrum. Of course, the more this happens the more he will think that this is what he can get away with.

How does a stepfather fit into a family structure? This was a question I had to answer. After all, I was not the biological dad, and my wife's kids were not "my kids." We talked and decided our best policy would be for her to make up the rules for her kids, and I would help her. Stepparents often are ignored, or if they participate in decision-making, they bump heads with the kids. I found that telling the kids that their mother was also my wife, helped clarify my position with them. They could appreciate the fact that I wasn't their dad, and wasn't making them do things because I replaced their dad; however, I am a person who is very interested in how people (including her kids) treat my wife. This seems to work for us.

Don't Be a One-Problem Parent

"My dog is fighting with my friend's dog and I need to stop him from doing this."

"You can bring him in for a class."

"Oh, he doesn't need a class, he is already trained."

"If he is trained, you can tell him 'lie down' when he starts getting aggressive."

"He wouldn't do it."

"In other words he knows what to do, but he won't do it."

"I don't like your attitude." Click.

Don't make the mistake of being a one-problem parent and thinking, "We don't care about the rest of that stuff, we just want our son to stop hitting his younger brother." This would be like saying, "You can kill people, set fires, and rob banks, but don't you dare put your muddy feet on the new sofa."

If your child respects you, and your family has a set of rules, your chance of solving one specific problem is good. Children behave better when they have a consistent set of rules to follow.

When I was nineteen, I joined the U.S. Air Force. I, like many other young men, joined because I wanted to get away from the rules at home. There are many reasons for joining the military, but the dumbest one is thinking that your parent's rules are worse than the military's rules.

As crazy as some of the military rules were, I learned a valuable lesson about following more than one rule. I learned the value of doing things that didn't always make sense. I was stationed at a training base that was divided into two parts. I lived on the new part of the base called the Triangle Area, and a mile away was the older Main Base. Our barracks had large lawns that had to be cut. Did we walk out the door and cut our own lawns? No, that would be too easy. We were split up into small groups and had to march a mile across the base to cut a lawn on the other side. As we marched along with our lawn mowers, we passed a group marching in the opposite direction to our side of the base to cut our lawn. We waved at the others, then joked and laughed at the stupidity of what we had to do. Anyone would know that cutting your own lawn would make more sense, but after a while I realized why we were made to do these activities.

After completing my training, I was told I had to go to Greenland for a year. This was the last thing I wanted to do, but I went. The lesson I learned was that getting people to do things (that may not make sense) is a great way to make sure that they will later do other things that may be more difficult and less enjoyable. As I mentioned earlier, going to Greenland turned out to be one of my most interesting experiences. Giving children, or adults, the chance to do new things that may not seem enjoyable, can open new doors for them.

As tempting as it may be to let everything slide except the one or two things we find important, we should understand that the key to solving individual behavior problems is to change the child's underlying attitude. We usually want to jump right in and address specific problems. If we are smart, we will change the underlying attitude first. The way to do this is to set up a number of expectations. You can succeed in changing your child's attitude by doing the things that don't seem to matter. The reason I went to Greenland was that I had been conditioned to do things that did not always seem to make sense. One of the ways we can do this is to give children responsibilities and make them do things that we could do for them.

Making your child do things when he would rather do something else is an excellent way of changing his attitude. Chores make sense for a number of reasons. They give the child the chance to learn how to do new things. They give the child the feeling of satisfaction of starting things on time and finishing them. They also lead to recognition for accomplishments, which fosters a desire to accomplish other things.

If we have a relationship with someone and we do everything for them, we aren't going to have much luck getting them to do things for themselves, or for us. Why should they?

This reminds me of a comment my forty-five-year-old cousin made to his ninety-three-year-old grandmother, who would trudge upstairs to his bedroom each morning to pick up his clothes and make his bed. She asked, "When are you going to learn to pick up your clothes?" and he jokingly replied, "Well, Gram, why should I learn when you have been doing it for me all of my life?"

✔ A parent's most important role is to create rules for your children to live by.

✔ Without structure your kids are not free, they are lost.

✔ Providing structure is your job.

✔ Without rules, there are just good or bad moods.

✔ Don't bend the rules, apply them or change them.

✔ Both parents should agree on, and enforce the rules.

✔ Sometimes it is appropriate to offer choices; other times certain behavior will be required.

✔ Giving kids choices does not mean they are adults.

✔ Kids don't fear requirements as much as we imagine.

✔ Don't lower the standard, raise the child.

✔ Teach your child your values and beliefs— don't expect him to make up his own.

✔ Don't be a one-problem parent.

Chapter Eight

The Three Meanings of "No"

S imple words can have several meanings and we must be careful not to create confusion. One fellow who came to my class with his dog explained that he was a mountain climber and that he used the word "down" to mean three different things: Lie down, go down the mountain, or get off what you are on. I wondered if the dog were on a mountain with his owner and was told, "Down," what would he do? Would he lie down, go down the mountain, or get off of it?

Never, Not Now, and Stop

The word "No" also can be confusing to a child. Here are some ideas that will help you teach your child exactly what you mean when you say "No."

"No" can mean at least three things: "Never do it," "Not now," or, "Stop doing what you are doing."

An example of "Never do it," is teaching your child not to stick anything in an electrical outlet. Another might be teaching your child never to get near your family dog while it is sleeping.

An example of "Not now," might be your answer to your child's request to go out and play during a thunderstorm. You tell your child that you don't want him out in the thunder and lightning, but you will let him go out and play when the weather clears up.

The third meaning, "Stop what you are doing," lets your child know that the activity he is doing was fine for a time, but has passed that point and it is time to stop. When I was a child, my aunt worked as a waitress in a restaurant and took me to work with her. Someone made the mistake of teaching me to play a little tune called "Chopsticks" on the piano. It is very repetitious. One day I stood in front of the piano in a restaurant and began to play for the people. At first they smiled at the little kid banging away at the piano. I am not sure how long I continued, it may have been only five or ten minutes, but some of the diners began to yell, "Thank you," and my aunt who had been busy going in and out of the kitchen told me that I had played enough for today. Her "No" did not mean that I could never play the song again, it meant, "Harold, you have played that song long enough, please stop what you are doing."

In each of these three examples we could use "No." We know which of the three meanings of "No" we mean, but will our children understand? Be specific and use "Never," "Not now," or "Stop what you are doing." The problem with using one word that can mean three things is that your child might find it hard to understand your exact meaning. If your child starts going out into the street and you tell him "No," you really mean, "Never go out in the street." If, twenty minutes later, your child asks for a cookie and you say, "No," you probably mean, "Not now, I don't want you to have a cookie before dinner." But if after dinner you allow your child to have a cookie, your child may think that "No" means "I can't do it now, but I can do it later," and might apply that to going out in the street. That is not what we want, is it?

Ask yourself this simple question, "Do I ever want my child doing this activity?" If your answer is, "I never want my child doing it," use the word "never." If your answer is, "I don't want my child doing it now, but I will permit it later," use the expression, "not now." If your answer is, "Yes, my child can do this, but when I tell him to stop, I want him to stop immediately," you can say, "Stop when I tell you," or simply, "Stop." The words are free and you can use the three different expressions to make it easier for your child to understand exactly which of the three ideas you mean.

Two students in my class called about their dog eating their stereo speaker. I invited them to come by to talk about their problem. When I asked them if their dog would eat the stereo when they were home, they said, of course their dog would not.

I asked what they would do if their dog tried to eat the speaker when they were home. They said they would tell the dog, "No."

Suddenly, a light came on in my brain. I finally understood why so many dog owners have trouble with the word "No."

What they had taught their dog was that she could go to the stereo speaker and they would tell her "No." They went to work one day and their dog went to the stereo speaker. She did not hear the word "No" because no one was home to say it. The dog chewed on the speaker.

"No" is such a simple word and it seems that we would find it easy to teach what it means. When we say, "No," and our child ignores us, we think our child is willfully disobedient. With some kids this is true, but it could be our child is confused by our misuse of the word "No."

Have you ever told your child, "No"? I'm sure you have. If it always worked, we'd be happy and all our kids would be well-behaved. When it doesn't work, we often say:

"No."

"I said 'No.'"

"I don't want to have to tell you 'No,' again."

"Didn't you hear me say 'No'?"

"No, and this time I really mean it."

Could it be our kids are doing a great job of learning, and that the trouble is that we just might be a little confused in our teaching? If you asked your daughter, "How much is $1 + 1$?" and she said, "3," you would think that she was not a good student. How would you feel if you saw her teacher telling her that $1 + 1 = 3$? You would think that while your daughter was good at learning, the problem was that her teacher couldn't add.

How many times have you heard a parent say, "No," and then watched the child ignore the word, or stop for a moment and then start right back up again?

Common Mistakes With the Word "No"

Not Knowing What We Are Teaching

We think we are teaching, "Never do it," while our kids are learning, "I can do something, you will catch me and say, 'No,' and I will stop for now." Confusion results when parents do not understand the difference between, "Stop when I tell you," and, "Never do it." If your child takes something he should not have, and you tell him "No" and fifteen minutes later he takes it again and you tell him "No" again, he is learning, "If you catch me I have to stop." The lesson you want your child to learn is, "Never do it." Kids take advantage of this loophole in the meaning of "No."

We Repeat Ourselves

We repeat the word "No" or we fail to follow through after we say the word "No." Children learn what a word means by first hearing it and then associating it with whatever happens. If we say "No," do nothing, and then repeat it, our children learn that the word "No" means nothing.

We Yell It Louder

If we don't succeed, we yell the word "No" louder. We teach our children that if they don't respond the first time, we will say it louder. This teaches them that they don't have to mind until we reach a certain volume. I am much more impressed when a child responds to a normal tone of voice. Do I ever believe in yelling? If there is a loud noise like a truck that will make it harder for me to be heard I may yell, but in general I like using my normal voice.

If there is a reason that your child may not hear you in an emergency, by all means, yell. I think however, that you and your children will be happier if they know that you say things once, and then follow through rather than yelling. You won't have to embarrass yourself by yelling and they won't have to listen to you yell.

Rewarding the Wrong Behavior

We might confuse a child by meaning and saying "No" while we reward the misbehavior. I was doing a school assembly with my dogs and watched a child talking with one of the other children. The nearest teacher told the child "No," and then had the child stand up and go to her and get hugged. This child may have needed more hugs, but the physical comforting of the hug outweighed the word "No." The lesson is that if you talk at a time when you should be listening, you get hugged.

We Expect Kids to Understand

We expect children to understand the deeper meaning of ordinary language.

Saying "No" is not the only way that we set limits for our children. We can mistakenly assume that children understand what certain words mean in the same way adults do. We took the kids to a Christmas buffet at a friend's house. We were the first to arrive, and after complimenting the host and hostess on the fabulous layout of food we were told, "Help yourselves." After we filled our plates, we sat with our friends while the kids went into the dining room, helped themselves, and sat in the other room eating. It turns out that our twelve-year-old zeroed in on the delicious Italian meatballs and while the rest of us took two or three, he scooped up fourteen of them. When he finished, he returned for another dozen. For adults "help yourself" means, "Take a few meatballs but remember that others might want some too." For a teenager it meant, "Take as many as you want."

We Cave in

If we have relatives visiting and one of them sees us stopping our child from doing something, she may say, "Oh, don't be so strict with him." When someone we love and respect talks us into bending our rules, we feel torn and we sometimes give in. If we do give in, for example, the child learns that when Grandma visits, the rules go out the window.

Not Everyone Thinks "No" Means "No"

We assume that everyone thinks "No" means "No." Depending on our past experiences, we each have an idea of what "No" means. Some of us have a very clear-cut sense that "No" means "No" and operate under the assumption that others think the same way that we do. This leads us to believe that when children (or people) are told "No," they will stop because they think that being told "No" is final. While many of us do stop when we hear "No," others ignore the word.

Imagine driving through a stop sign and being stopped by a police officer. The officer tells you, "No, don't go running stop signs," and then releases you. What would you think?

If you are a model citizen, it might frighten you enough to get you to stop at stop signs. Suppose, however, that a criminal who has been through the judicial system (including prison) was treated the same way for going through the stop sign. Since being told "No" would be nothing compared to his past experience, he would laugh and think, "Today is my lucky day, I got away with it."

In fact, if you learned that the worse thing that would happen to you would be that you would be stopped and told "No," you might begin to think that you could drive through stop signs without any real penalty.

This brings up the question, "Why isn't being told 'No' always a big negative consequence?" The answer is that "No" is only as negative to us as our reaction to the consequence that follows. What really counts is what we think will happen after the word "No" is used. If the criminal who has been in prison does something wrong and is told "No" it will not be a very significant, negative experience. If we take pride in obeying the law and are told "No" by a police officer, it triggers a stronger emotional response of fear and guilt.

Once He Knows, Skip the Reminders and Warnings

I watched a television program featuring a story about a dog trainer who handled dog complaints for a city. People would go to him instead of court, and the dog trainer would discuss the person's dog violation and give some suggestions for helping the person solve the dog's behavior problem.

As the trainer was lecturing the dog owner on the importance of making effective corrections, the trainer's dog got up from a down-stay. The trainer shouted, "No!" in a loud voice, then turned to the owner and said emphatically, "Now, that is a correction." I thought, "No, it is not, it is a reminder."

Once your child understands that a certain activity is a "Never," be smart and don't fall into the habit of reminding and warning your child.

When you are teaching, you can repeat the lesson again and again, and you can remind and warn what the consequence will be if your child ignores the lesson. However, once your child knows what "never" means, don't remind or warn your child. If your child respects the limit, good. If not, switch to the negative consequence you have set up in advance.

Why not repeat the words "No" or "Never" as warnings and reminders once your child knows and understands that an activity is a never? Here are three reasons:

1. *Your child may have to deal with this situation when he is alone and you are not there to repeat the warning.*

2. *Your child may keep testing you by misbehaving because he knows you will warn him before he will receive a correction from you.*

3. *If your child starts to ignore the rule and responds to your warning, what do you do? Should you correct him for ignoring the rule, or praise him for responding to your warning? This puts you in the awkward position of not knowing what you are doing.*

You can stop this confusion by not giving reminders and warnings. For your child's benefit, you shouldn't have to repeat yourself.

Teach a Positive, Substitute Behavior

"When my dog jumps on me I tell him 'No,' but he keeps doing it. How do you get him to stop jumping?"

"Teach him to sit and stay. A dog can't sit and stay, and jump up at the same time."

The opposite of "Never" is "Always," and another excellent way to teach your child what he should not do is to teach him what he should do. Rather than teaching, "Never go in the street," teach your child, "Always stay on the sidewalk."

Teaching your child a positive, substitute behavior has several advantages over teaching not to do something. You might laugh at the things kids do when told not to do something. A child runs past a parent who shouts, "Don't run in the house." Minutes later the child skips by and the parent yells, "I told you not to run in the house." "I'm not running, I'm skipping." "Well, no skipping in the house." Finally, the child hops on one foot past the parent. The parent could yell, "No running, no skipping, no hopping, no three-legged racing, no jumping on two feet, no bouncing off the walls." You will have more success by telling your child what to do.

Instead of telling your child, "Don't run in the house," tell your child, "Sit down and read your book."

As we can see from the above example with the child running, if we just stop a negative behavior, we often leave the door open for other negative behavior. A better approach is to teach the child to do something acceptable. If the child who runs, skips, and hops is told, "Sit down and read your book," it gives the child a very specific action to take.

One advantage is that it is easier to accomplish a positively stated goal. If I get in my car and say, "I am going to Portland," I will be much more likely to get there, than if I get in my car and think, "I don't want to go to Seattle, and I don't want to go to Sacramento."

Another advantage is that it is easier to judge whether your child is doing what you say. You can easily see that your child is sitting and reading a book. This allows the third advantage, which is that once your child is seen reading the book, you can acknowledge the good behavior and praise your child.

The Best Way to Teach the Concept "No" Is Not to Use the Word

Many of us approach a behavior problem by yelling and screaming, "No!" Some kids may respond out of fear, but yelling and being angry are really signals that we lack control and feel helpless. You can improve your child's behavior and your relationship with your child by realizing that the best way to teach the concept "No" is to stop yelling the word.

Replace yelling with action. Drop the word "No" for one week. Teach positive, substitute behaviors, and if that doesn't work, use negative consequences to correct unwanted behavior. You, your child, and the people around you will be happier when you reach the point where you will not need to constantly yell, "No!"

This does not mean that we overlook bad behavior and throw our rules out the window. It means that when we catch our child doing something wrong, we deal with it and then we pull the child back on track by pointing out and demanding the right behavior.

✔ The word "No" has three different meanings. Choose your words so that your meaning is clear.

✔ Even if you aren't aware of it, you are teaching all the time.

✔ Repeating yourself teaches your child not to listen.

✔ Just yelling louder doesn't get results.

✔ Don't reward the wrong behavior.

✔ Don't expect kids to understand if you are not specific and clear.

✔ Don't cave in to pressure.

✔ Understand, and teach, the three meanings of "No"—stop immediately, not now, never.

✔ Once your child knows what he is supposed to do, skip the reminders and warnings.

✔ Teach a positive, substitute behavior.

Chapter Nine

Customize Your Parenting

For my first thirty-nine years, I believed that everyone thought the way I did. Because I believed we all thought the same way, I wondered why others did things that I would never do. Some of the things they did were better than my best, and some of the things they did were worse than I would ever do. I felt like I was walking around the streets of Seattle with a map of New York in my hand. After I opened my dog training school, I realized that I needed some help with my people skills. One of the most important ideas I ever learned is, "We are all different, and we all think that we are right."

Once I looked at everyone's behavior with these ideas in mind, I became much better at getting along with people, and more skilled at helping others. You can do this, too, without sacrificing your integrity. Best of all, you also increase your chances of getting what you want.

What does this have to do with parenting? If you want to be a more effective parent, you must understand that your kids are individuals, and the parenting techniques that worked with you may not work with them. Your job is to discover what will work with each of your children and customize your approach.

Before taking a class or reading a book about parenting, we look to our past for ideas. Our parents are the most logical and likely source of the ideas we use with our kids. If you liked your parents' ideas, you will use them. If you didn't like what your parents did, you may decide to do just the opposite. If your parents were oppressive, you might be far less structured. You might think, "I don't want my kid to undergo what I went through." This could mean that we think, "I don't want my child to turn out like I did." I know that I thought that way when I decided not to have kids and it wasn't until I fell in love with someone who had kids, that I changed my mind. I don't think there is anything wrong with learning from our experiences as we grew up and avoiding the problems we had as kids. In the chapter on worrying, you learned that one of my concerns as a parent is to avoid the excessive worrying that I grew up with.

It May Not Work With Your Kids

What happens when we think, "What worked with me will work with my kids"? If your parent yelled at you, you may yell when you discipline your child. If isolation (time out, which used to be called, "Go to your room,") worked on you, you may use it. The same is true with verbal humiliation, spanking, or whatever your parents did to you.

When what we do actually works, we are happy. What happens when it doesn't work? We think, "I've tried everything and nothing works." We may have tried everything we know, but that is usually not everything that is available. There are other ideas we can use to be more effective parents.

Don't Wait to Get Help

Often, we hold onto our own ideas, even when they don't work. We don't seek help until we have serious problems. I once talked to a friend who struggled with her dog for three years before she finally sought help. I asked her why she waited so long and she said that she was a schoolteacher and felt that she had enough experience with training that she didn't need to seek help.

I thought of what I do when my car doesn't run. I open the hood, look under it, close it, and take it to my mechanic. I suppose I would feel differently if I tried to fix my car for three years before giving up and taking it in.

Find Out What Is Important to Your Kids

Once we change from thinking that everyone thinks like we do, we ask, "What is important to our kids?" Some respond to words of praise or criticism, and others couldn't care less. Some respond to isolation while others enjoy solitude.

One day, I was doing a talk for an organization and someone mentioned that he had a fear of getting up in front of an audience. He asked me how I had overcome my fear of public speaking and I jokingly told him that I had replaced my fear of being in front of the audience with a fear of being in the audience.

When I was a kid, every second sentence out of my mouth was, "Can I go out?" What I find funny now is that when I visit a friend, his son always hides in his room. We sit outside in the backyard, and he hides in his room. Keeping me in the house when I was a kid was a negative consequence, but indoor isolation will not work with my friend's son because he loves being in his room.

Don't Fall Into the "Why" Trap

In the following two examples, these dog owners focus on "why" they are having a problem and have no interest in solving the behavior.

"We're going to get rid of our dog for barking, and we want to know why he barks."

"I can help you stop the barking."

"No, we have already decided to get rid of him and we just wanted to know why he barks."

The second dog owner wanted to know why her dog had suddenly become fearful and was panicking. The dog was afraid of her and her friends. She said, "I don't know why, my friends don't know why, and I want a dog psychologist to tell me why." I told her I had experience helping people with fearful dogs.

She said, "I don't want help, I want to know why. No thanks."

If your child were sick and your child's doctor diagnosed the problem, then smiled and said, "I am happy to tell you that I found out why your child is sick. Thanks for coming in." You might wonder what the why was, but I am sure you would be much more concerned with another question, "What can you do to help my child?"

As we look at what is important to the child, we don't want to get stuck in the "why" trap.

There may be times to wonder, "Why?" but there are also times when you have to act. If your house is on fire, how much time will you spend wondering, "Why did my house catch on fire?" You might spend a fraction of a second, and then think about getting yourself and your loved ones out as fast as possible.

Knowing Why May Be the First Step, but Not the Last

There are times when knowing why something is happening helps us solve a problem or prevents it from happening again.

There are parents who wander from one child counselor to another and one parenting book to another, searching for the reason why. They become consumed in finding why while they fail to focus on solving the problem. There are times when we find out why and it doesn't do us any good. Once we discover why a child is doing something, we should figure out what to do about it.

Finding the Label Isn't Solving the Problem

Along with getting stuck in the why of the problem, some of us stop after we discover the label. Once an expert labels the behavior with an official-sounding name, we feel we have dealt with the behavior. Saying that our child has Attention Deficit Disorder (ADD) allows us to think we have done something.

Don't stop there and just use the ADD label as an explanation for everything your child does: "My child flunked math because of ADD;" "My child was late for class because of ADD;" "My child shoplifts because of ADD." I am not saying this condition is unimportant, but we should find out how to help our child rather than just stamping our child's problems with a label.

Turn "Why" into Action

Once you find out why, start doing something about it. It may be difficult to understand why children and adults do what they do, particularly when they do things that strike us as totally wrong. Whenever you are looking for explanations (and have ruled out medical problems), yet can't come up with a reasonable (or unreasonable) explanation, just realize: they are doing it because they want to.

This may seem ridiculously simplistic, but this answer helps you move to your next step which is: how am I going to deal with this behavior? This makes for less interesting conversation, but will help you get to the next step much faster than speculating about why he does it.

If we assume that kids and people do things because they want to, we don't waste a lot of time speculating on motives they themselves may not even know. Instead, we can establish a foundation that helps us develop strategies for dealing with their behavior. If we want them to change, we need to figure out what is important to them rather than what would work with us.

Don't Take Misbehavior Personally

"My dog misbehaves because he hates me."

It is perfectly natural to think that dogs and kids misbehave either because they don't like us, or they want to spite us. One idea has made my life a lot easier. As I mentioned earlier, I find it helpful not to take a child's misbehavior personally.

Once we assume that children do things because they want to, we might take the next step and wonder, "Why is my child doing this to me?" It is even easier to think this when your child acts one way with you and another way with the other parent. When we look at it as, "My child is doing something because he wants to do it, whether it makes me happy or not," it helps us solve the problem, rather than involving our emotions to help us get revenge for deliberately spiteful behavior.

Expressing Your Feelings

One popular idea about getting someone to change their behavior is to "express your feelings." Expressing your feelings makes you feel better, but you can't always rely on it to cause others to change their behavior. This idea assumes that others care enough about your feelings to change their behavior.

What happens if your child cares more about her feelings than yours? I saw an interesting example of this while visiting a family at their apartment. The teenage daughter wanted to go out at 10:30 at night to do her laundry at the other end of the apartment complex. First, her mother told her she didn't think it was smart for her to go out that late, but her daughter just kept picking up her clothing. Her mother continued, "I really don't feel comfortable about this at all." I could hear the daughter going through her purse for change for the washer and dryer. After her mother finally said, "I feel upset that you are ignoring me," I heard the door open and close as the daughter left. I thought, "So much for the effectiveness of expressing your feelings."

Expressing your feelings to your spouse may work if your spouse cares about your feelings. It may also work with your children, but I am sure that you have seen a child act with total insensitivity to a parent's feelings. The child thinks, "My feelings about getting what I want are far more important to me than my parent's feelings about my not having what I want."

Please understand, I am not suggesting keeping your feelings bottled up inside of you, that is not emotionally healthy; however, some of us think that expressing feelings is the only alternative to burying your feelings, and being stepped on and ignored by others. Fortunately, this isn't true. If expressing your feelings works, do it.

When you shift from thinking that your child will respond to you because he wants to make you happy, and realize that your child's main interest is in what makes him happy, you are on the road to being a more effective parent.

This does not mean that you devote your life to making your child happy by doing everything for him and giving him everything he wants. It means you present information, including your requests and demands, in a way that gets your child to think that going along with your ideas will benefit him, rather than just making you happy.

Remember, we are all different and we all think we are right.

✔ Customize your approach with each child, rather than treating all of your kids the way your parents treated you.

✔ What your parents did to raise you may not work with your kids.

✔ Don't wait to get help.

✔ Find out what is important to your child.

✔ Don't fall into the "why" trap.

✔ Knowing "why" may be the first step, but it is not the last.

✔ Finding the label isn't solving the problem.

✔ One answer to, "Why does he do it?" may be, "Because he likes to."

✔ Don't take misbehavior personally.

✔ Expressing your feelings may not be enough to persuade your kids.

Chapter Ten

Saying It Once

Say it once and follow through. Making this one easy change will put you miles ahead of where you are now.

> *"How many times do you want to call your dog if he is out in the street and a truck is coming?"*
>
> *I have never had a person say, "I'd like to have to call my dog more than one time."*
>
> *If you want your dog to come the first time you call, you must teach your dog, "I say it once, and expect you to respond the first time I say it."*

If we want our child to respond the first time we say something, we must teach that we mean it the first time we say it.

You might be wondering, "How can I tell my child something just once and expect my child to understand what I am expecting? Don't I have to repeat things, so my child will understand?" You might be confused about repeating what you are teaching, and repeating yourself.

You may have heard, "Repetition is the mother of learning." This is true when we repeat lessons such as:

> "1 + 1 = 2. How much is 1 + 1?"
> "2."
> "Good. Now how much is 1 + 1?"
> "2."
> "That's right."

In this case, we repeat a lesson until repetition becomes the mother of learning.

What happens when we tell a child to do something, he ignores us, and we tell him again? In this case, repetition is the mother of learning the wrong thing, if we repeat ourselves and don't follow through.

Here is an example of the wrong lesson being learned:

> Two kids are outside playing.
> One kid's parent calls out, "Billy."
> Billy continues playing.
> Billy's playmate asks, "Aren't you going home, Billy?"
> Billy laughs and says, "No I don't have to go home until the fifth yell."

Billy knows that his parent is a "five" which means he knows that the first four times don't count.

Ask Them, Tell Them, Make Them, or Say It Once and Follow Through

A police officer on television said that she was trained to ask first, then tell, and then make the person she is dealing with comply with her request. In my dog training classes, we simply say it once and then follow through, but if you want to use the three-step approach, do it. Once you set your pattern, stick with it. Skip the threats and warnings. Ask them, tell them, make them, or say it once and then follow through.

Repeat Lessons, But Don't Repeat Yourself

The idea of saying it once and then following through applies to any word or idea that you are teaching your child.

This is difficult for some of us because we feel that by repeating ourselves we are being kind and giving our children a better chance to learn things. The opposite is true. We are being unfair to teach our children they don't have to respond the first time we say something, but we will get mad at them for not listening to us. I believe that kids are always learning what we are teaching, whether we think we are teaching or not. This may include the fact that we don't mean what we say.

Some parents repeat themselves and then wonder why their children don't respond the first time. Repeating ourselves may be a difficult habit to break.

Here is how I make sure that I don't repeat myself when I work with dogs in my dog class. I invite my students to catch me saying something more than once to my dog, their dog, or another student's dog (except when I am praising). Anyone who hears me repeat a word to a dog can come over, kick me, and collect $10, and then tell everyone else in the class, then all of them can kick me and also collect $10. No one has collected yet. The first night I get caught I will quit teaching dog training classes.

Let your child know that you don't want to nag him by telling him over and over again, and if he catches you saying something more than once without following through, you will give him a reward. You might also add that when you say something once, you expect your child to respond. While this may encourage your child to test you at the beginning, your child will eventually realize that you say things only once and then follow through. This also teaches your child to avoid putting things off by learning the very important lesson of saying something once, and then doing what you say.

True, But Irrelevant Statements

Don't pound your child over the head with true, but irrelevant, statements.

These include, "I told you we are leaving and to get in the car," after you told your child, "We are leaving, get in the car." This statement is true, but it is irrelevant.

Next we have, "Didn't you hear me tell you we are leaving?" and the follow-up threat, "I am going to tell you one more time."

Finally we get to the statement, "This time I really mean it," which of course shouts out to the child that we didn't mean any of the rest of what we said.

Talk Less and Act More

If your child will not respond unless you say things over and over, you are talking too much and doing too little. If your child will not respond unless you yell in a loud voice, say it once (quietly) and then follow through.

Remember Billy who knew his parent would say things five times before he had to respond? Don't be a "five" like his parent; be a "one." Say it once, and then act.

Even if you ignore all of the other ideas in this book, follow this one suggestion. You will be amazed at how much better your relationship with your child will be.

✔ Nags, threats, and warnings won't be
necessary anymore.

✔ Say it once and follow through.

✔ Repeat lessons, but don't repeat yourself.

✔ Break your habit of repeating yourself by
offering a reward if your kids catch you.

Chapter Eleven

Parent as Teacher

Teaching is one of our most important jobs. As someone who taught school, I can appreciate the challenges teachers have as they teach a group of students. Schoolteachers teach children, test them, and then the students move on to a different class. Parental teaching differs from teaching students at school because when we teach, we communicate new information to our children, persuade them to use the information, and then live daily with the success or failure of our efforts.

The Difference Between Teaching and Training

> "My dog knows what to do, but he won't do it."
> "At least you have done a good job of teaching your dog, now all you have to do is train him."

In this chapter you will learn how to be a better teacher.

Teaching helps your child know what to do. Once your child knows what to do, your second job is to follow through and make sure that your child does what he is supposed to do. That is training. I can think of four ways we teach our children life's lessons and persuade them to follow through.

Teach by Example

The first way is teaching by example. We must watch the difference between what we say and what we do because we can be sure that our children will be watching any difference between our words and our actions. If we tell our children to follow rules, but break our own rules (like running a red light), our children get a mixed message. Children are always learning, whether we think we are teaching or not, and whether we know what we are teaching or not.

Use an Emotional Appeal

The second is an emotional appeal based on love and charisma. We assume our children will do what we want just because they want to please us. We assume that our children will follow our advice because they love and care about us as parents. If you recall the example in chapter nine involving the girl caring more about wanting to do her laundry than her mother's feelings, you realize that appealing to your child's love and caring about your feelings doesn't always work.

Use Power

The third approach is based on power. If we are teaching our child to stay out of the street and the child refuses, we can pick him up and take him to safety. We also can use our power to hold back allowances, place a child in time out, or remove television privileges. If telling the child not to watch television doesn't work, we can physically remove the child from the television, or the television from the child. Some of us may worry that using our power will break our child's spirit. Good parenting doesn't break a child's spirit, it channels and directs it so that the child can grow up and reach his potential.

Appeal to Self-Interest

The fourth approach is appealing to your child's self-interest. This is more than just telling your child what to do. That would be using your power; although there is nothing wrong with using your power when other approaches don't work. If you feel uncomfortable arguing and fighting with your child about why he should learn something, this fourth approach will help. I am sure you will find it both comfortable and effective. I call this approach the "You" focus. Before I learned how to use the "You" focus, I used the "I" focus.

The Difference Between the "You" Focus and the "I" Focus

Imagine you are in a parenting class and you hear the teacher start the class in one of the following two ways. Which sounds most interesting to you?

1. *This is week two and the topic I am going to cover tonight is the word "No."*

2. *This is your week-two class and you are going to learn how to use the word "No" more effectively. Once you understand that the word "No" has three meanings, your child will find it easier to understand what you mean when you say, "No."*

Chances are, you find the second far more interesting. Why? In the first statement you only hear what the teacher is going to do. You are not even mentioned. In the second statement, you first hear what you are going to learn, and then you hear that your knowledge will help your child understand what you want him to do. Whether you are communicating with your child or anyone else, using this "You" makes you a far more effective teacher.

The Power of Self-Interest

If you had taken my dog class back in 1976 when I started, you would have heard me talk like the teacher in example #1. Several years later, I discovered one of the most valuable ideas I ever learned in my life.

Most of the time people are thinking about themselves.

If you want others to pay attention to you, you should say something that is important to them, rather than what is important to you. I use this approach in my classes, and with people who call on the phone about their dogs. Not only does this help me be a better teacher, it also helps me be a better parent, and a better listener. You will be more skilled as a parent once you understand and use this simple approach to teaching.

Use the Camera to Help You With the "You" Focus

At first, I had a hard time changing from talking about myself. I kept slipping back into "I" statements. What helped me change was to pretend to be a photographer holding a camera and taking a picture. You, the parent, are holding the camera. You can point the camera so that it focuses on yourself, the subject, your child, or a combination of the three.

In the first example above, you see that the teacher is focusing the camera on himself and the subject. In the second example, you see that the camera is focused first on you, then the subject (the word "No"), and finally your child. When you teach your child, aim the camera so it focuses on your child and the subject. You do this by using the words "you" and "your" to link your child and the subject.

The "We" Focus

There are times when including others by using "we" works and other times when it sounds phony. With "we" talk, you focus the camera on your child, the subject, and yourself. Have you ever gone to the doctor and had the nurse ask, "How are we feeling today?" or, "How much do we weigh today?" That sounds condescending to me. I am tempted to say, "Well I am about 200 pounds, and you look about 130 pounds, which adds up to 330." I'm not sure what the nurse is thinking when she says "we," because the nurse and I are obviously not a "we" in the same sense that you and your child are when you say, "We are going to get some ice cream." If your child accepts the concept of "we," then use "we" talk, and if it doesn't work, switch back to "you" talk.

What's in It for Me?

This is not just telling your child, "You should clean your room." While this does put your child and the subject (a clean room) in the picture together, it lacks the other important element, which is self-interest. To appeal to your child's self-interest, think about the question your child is asking, which is, "What's in it for me?"

The big advantage to you when you first start using the "you" focus, is that you can see how effective it is. By concentrating on using what is important to your children, you get them to do what you want them to do. This does not mean that you always let your children have their way, particularly if it goes against what you know is best.

If you want your child to change, base your appeal on what your child thinks is important. To keep you interested in this book, I write not only about my experiences, but how these experiences might relate to you and your child. I'm sure that you are far more interested in what these ideas mean to you, rather than just reading about my experiences as a dog trainer who became a stepfather.

The Benefit

The second part of the "you" focus is the benefit, which means getting your children to see the value to themselves in doing what you want them to do. We must understand how important it is to combine the two ideas: "We are all different and we all think that we are right," and, "Most of the time people are concerned with themselves."

Imagine for a moment that you and your spouse go to buy a car. You dress well, while your spouse is more casual. You want a car that looks good and has extra safety features, and you don't mind paying a little more if you can get something that is more attractive. Your spouse on the other hand is less concerned about appearance, and is more concerned about roominess and price. If the salesperson talks to you both about how much room the car has and the economical price, you might not be as interested as if the appearance and safety features are brought to your attention. Keep this example in mind when you talk with your child. Your reasons for having your children do something may have little appeal to them, unless you know what is important to them.

Some might consider this trickery or manipulation. It isn't. Think of it this way—your job is to persuade your child. Doesn't it make more sense to learn how to be more persuasive than to use the trial-and-error method where you make it up as you go along? Of course it does. In fact, not paying attention to what others care about diminishes them and makes it difficult to get our ideas across. We can't assume that because something is important to us that our children will feel the same way.

By using questions, you can find out what is important to your child. When your child makes a judgmental statement about someone or something, use that chance to find out what your child thinks. Ask what makes someone or something "cool" or "gross." Your child's answer tells you a lot about what he thinks. You can then use this information when you talk about other things with your child.

Teaching and persuading are important parts of parenting. As you perfect this "you" focus and its benefit, you will feel even more competent as a parent.

Assume That Your Child Will Learn

"You are going to find this easy to learn."
"You are going to find this hard to learn."

If you were a child, which statement would like to hear before you started doing something new? Help your child learn by saying that something is easy, rather than the material is hard, even if it is difficult. You probably know people who say they know they are going to have a hard time learning something, and guess what, they do have a hard time.

You set the tone for your child. If you scare him by pointing out how difficult something will be, he will believe you. Set the stage by saying, "You are going to have fun learning how to stay on the sidewalk, and once you know how, you will be able to play outside with your friends by yourself." In this sentence, you focus on your child enjoying the experience, and you highlight the benefit of learning this lesson.

Teach How to Do It

Don't just tell your child to do something and then be disappointed if he does it wrong. Teach what to do and how to do it. You have no doubt seen and heard of volumes of "How To" books. One of the smartest things I have done to improve my life has been to look at life as a "How To" project. I am amazed at how much information is available to help us deal with many of life's complexities. The advantage of looking at life as a "How To" project is that you look at what you are doing, set goals, and then take steps to reach them. You realize you are not just a cork bouncing around on the ocean. Others have had the same problem and some have figured out what to do about it. You don't have to reinvent the wheel.

After you start looking at parenting as a "How To" project, you will be a better teacher for your child. Instead of just reacting to situations, you will ask yourself, "What does my child have to know how to do so he can handle peer group pressure (or any other problem) at school?"

Be Specific

One expression that many of us tell our kids is, "Be careful." A friend of mine told me it used to drive him crazy when his mother would tell him to be careful. He once asked what "Be careful" meant and his mother said it meant to stay on the sidewalk. He said, "So when I start driving, you want me to drive on the sidewalk?" Giving children vague directions such as, "Be careful," or even worse, "Don't get into trouble," requires them to figure out what "trouble" is and then not do it. This makes it hard for them to know exactly what we mean. Be specific.

How Kids Learn What Words Mean

> "When my dog jumps up, I tell him, 'Get down,' but he keeps jumping up. It seems the more I tell him, the more he does it."
>
> "It could be that your dog has learned that the words 'Get down' mean 'Jump up.'"
>
> "How could he be so stupid?"
>
> "Dogs learn what words mean by connecting an action with a word or phrase. If your dog jumps up and you say, 'Get down,' your dog might think that 'Get down' means 'Jump up.'"

Children also learn in this manner—by connecting an action with a word or phrase.

When we were babies our parents pointed to themselves and said, "Mama," or, "Papa." This taught us what the words meant. As we moved around the house and touched things, we learned that some things are chairs, dogs, or tables. What would happen if your mother pointed at herself and said, "Frying pan"? You would think that the words "frying pan" described your mother. We would find it strange if our parents called themselves things like frying pan, but are we doing that with our children? Yes, if we say something and don't follow through. For example, our child might learn that, "Do your homework," really means you can go into your room, watch television, and call up your friends, instead of actually doing your homework. Remember, kids learn from what actually happens, not just what we think they should learn.

Don't Expect Kids to Know Things

We had an experience where another adult asked the kids a question and they answered the question honestly, even though we thought the information was none of the other person's business. At first, we felt annoyed that the kids talked without thinking, but we decided it wasn't their fault because we had not told them to keep what they heard confidential.

You Are Doing It Wrong

I used to teach by pointing out all of the mistakes that my students made. While some people learned from my negative comments, I found that others would continue making the same mistakes. Rather than telling them they are doing it wrong, I now tell them what to do, and they do much better in class.

Let's say you are teaching your child to look both ways before crossing the street and you see him look only one way and then start into the street. You could say, "You did it wrong, you only looked one way," or you could say, "When you step out, look both ways." In the second sentence, you let him know he didn't do it right and you also tell him what to do. Teach your child what to do, rather than telling him what he is doing wrong.

Sorry, 1 + 1 Does Not = 3

You may have heard that some school children are being taught that it is OK to think that 1 + 1 = 3 because how they feel about themselves is more important than knowing how to add 1 + 1. Some people are concerned that grading children and telling them they don't know the right answer might cause them emotional problems. On the other hand, 1 + 1 does not equal 3, and sending a child out into the world with high self-esteem but without the ability to add, is like putting frosting on an unbaked cake.

I had a hard time with math in high school. In trigonometry at mid-term, I got a grade of 40 out of 100 and that was only because the teacher didn't give a grade lower than 40. I think that my average was actually 28. I was completely lost and really had to scramble to get up to a passing grade of 65. I was never asked, "Harold, how do you feel about trigonometry or your ability to do trigonometry?" I didn't suffer any emotional damage because others in class got a 98 and I got a 40. In fact, I did get some useful feedback that prevented me from pursuing trigonometry as a career, and I also learned that I would probably never be very good at measuring flagpoles (which is, as I understand it, the major advantage for the average person to learn trigonometry).

I believe that my school did me a favor. Letting me drift along with the false idea that I was good at trigonometry would have been a far greater cruelty than the momentary embarrassment I felt as the teacher went around the room asking us to guess our grades. She then announced our grades in front of everyone. There was less concern for our feelings than our performance, although we did feel good when we passed the course. We were rewarded not just for being there, but for learning the subject.

Keep Pulling Them Back onto the Right Track

There is right and wrong when you are testing, but while teaching, we want to focus on doing it right because it makes it easier to learn something when you are more concerned with doing it correctly, rather than not doing something wrong. Once the child knows and understands what we have taught, and we test the child, we can think in terms of right or wrong. We can evaluate whether or not our child learned the lesson properly. Obviously, our kids don't always get things right when they are learning something new. The point here is that while your child is not always right, no one likes to be wrong or stupid while learning something new.

Here is an idea I find helpful. When you start to teach something, you have to know two things. First, you have to know what you are teaching. Second, you have to know how you will be sure your child has learned the lesson. I like to think of it as getting on a train and reaching a destination. You have to know which city you are going to, and how you will tell you are there. There are times when lessons go off-track, either accidentally or deliberately, but by using the idea of keeping the train on track and reaching your destination, you are more likely to notice any detours. The idea of staying on track also helps you get the child back to the lesson more easily.

How to Keep Them on Track

One approach you might use is to talk about the future. Let's say that your child accidentally spills a glass of milk because he was looking at the milk in the glass rather than where he was walking. Instead of saying either, "You spilled the milk," which is pretty obvious, or, "Don't spill the milk again," teach your child how to do it the right way. "When you walk across the room again with a glass of milk, it is easier if you look where you are going instead of looking at the glass." This does not ignore your child's mistakes, but it does allow him to do it better the next time without concentrating on not spilling.

The reason this works is that when kids are told not to do something, they have to think about what they are not supposed to do and then avoid doing it. Thinking about what they should not do reinforces the image of what not to do. It then requires an additional step of not doing it. It also creates the emotional responses of stupidity and failure involved with being "wrong," rather than the positive image of doing something right. This is not the same thing as letting a child believe that 1+1 = 3. You can correct children by teaching them what to do and how to do it, rather than by telling them, "Don't do it wrong." Give your child credit for doing whatever part of the task was done properly and then use a link that moves the child into the future and doing it again the right way.

By linking the right way to do it with either time or improved results, you let your child know, "You didn't get it completely right that time, and if you make this change you will improve next time."

You can use one of these expressions:

1. *Do it again, but this time...*

2. *When you do it again, do it...*

3. *In the future...*

4. *You can do it faster if you...*

5. *It is easier to do it if you...*

Help your child feel right about any part of what is being done correctly, and add the new suggestion as an afterthought. "You held the glass of milk with two hands which was very good, and all you need to do the next time is to look where you are walking."

Do Realistic Testing

"I'm just calling to let you know we can't come to class tonight because Lady is in heat."

"That's no problem."

"I thought it might upset the male dogs."

"It might, but that's their problem."

"Isn't that unfair?"

"Testing your dog with realistic distractions is the only way to know if your dog is reliable."

After you think that your child has learned what you are teaching, be sure to test. Make the test realistic.

You have no doubt seen the disturbing set-ups on television where a parent has talked to a child about not going off with strangers. The parent is then shown a video of the child walking off with one.

Fortunately, the child is safe. These tests are staged to alert parents that just talking to your child and getting him to say, "Yes," when you ask, "Do you understand that you are not supposed to walk off with strangers?" is not enough. A more realistic test is one where a friend of yours (someone your child does not know) asks your child to go with him. Make the test as hard as or harder than real-life.

Don't make the serious mistake of feeling, "I wouldn't do that to my child, it might upset him." Your friend doing the test is not going to harm your child, and even if your child flunks the test, you are not going to cause harm by criticizing. Instead, look at it as valuable information that tells you whether or not you can rely on your child to make the right decision. If your child fails the test, get back to teaching the lesson again until your child can pass the test.

While you are teaching your child skills like staying on the sidewalk, you also are teaching what I like to call life lessons. You are teaching your child what to do when things go right and when things go wrong—when they have successes and when they have problems. You also are teaching patience and determination. Everything you do counts and the more you know about teaching, the better your child will do as he learns about life.

How to Improve Your Teaching

Take a short class in something you know little about. Get a sense of the difference between a good teacher and a not-so-good teacher. Check to see if the teacher talks more about himself and the subject, or if he gets you involved.

At the suggestion of a friend who owned a real estate office, I took a course to get my license in real estate sales. While I enjoy living in a house, I didn't find real estate very interesting. I completed the course and I passed the exam, but the best part of the experience for me was the great teacher, Norman Webb; because instead of just talking about tax lots and trust deeds, he put his students in the picture. While I found the information boring, I really looked forward to attending his classes. By the time I took his class, I had taught high school for two years and dog classes for five years. I realized how much more there was to teaching than simply talking about the subject and myself.

If you want to become a better teacher, or just sharpen your teaching skills, remember to put your child in the picture and tie your lessons to a benefit to your child.

Learn How to Persuade Your Child

Being persuasive is part of parenting. We have to do it whether we know what we are doing or not. The question is, "How can we become more persuasive?"

My suggestion is to take a course, read books, or buy a good audio cassette program that teaches you how to sell. While I certainly value my six-year experience getting my master's degree, I learned far more about human relations from a five-day course in sales training. I am not suggesting that you become a salesperson. What I am suggesting is that you learn ethical selling. Ethical selling involves helping people make decisions that are good for them. A sales training course teaches you the value of asking questions, and listening, and then using this information to help your children make decisions that are good for them.

I was once at the top of the list of people who said, "I could never sell anything." Looking back at it, this is a pretty silly statement for someone who is a teacher. All parents and schoolteachers should learn how to sell and persuade. That's our job.

✔ You may feel uncomfortable pushing your values onto your child, or you may feel you don't know how to teach. Don't confuse teaching with training.

✔ Focus on the child's point of view to engage his self-interest.

✔ State the benefit to your child in a clear way he can understand.

✔ Assume that your child will learn.

✔ Teach what to do, rather than what not to do.

✔ Don't just tell them what to do, teach them how to do it.

✔ Kids learn what words mean by seeing what happens when they hear a word.

✔ Don't expect kids to know what they haven't been taught.

✔ Instead of saying, "You are doing it wrong," give positive reinforcement then point out how to improve the performance next time.

✔ Be a better teacher by learning how to persuade your child.

Chapter Twelve

Training and Discipline

Once your child knows what is expected, your next job as a parent is to help your child live within the guidelines. This involves dealing with two issues. The first is finding out what will work with each child. The second is overcoming our reluctance to discipline. Let's look at some of the reasons why we have problems with this important issue. One reason is that we don't follow through. We begin with great enthusiasm and then start coasting and give up. Why don't we follow through?

We Don't Think It Is Important

> *"I started your class with our dog and quit after two weeks because it didn't seem important. Then, our dog bit our child and now it is very important that we get the dog trained. I want to bring him back to class."*

Some of us procrastinate and don't do what we know we should do with our children. We start something, get lulled into a sense of security, and then reality hands us a wake-up call.

Don't make the mistake this parent made by overlooking what didn't seem important.

In the chapter on planning, we learned to be smart by planning before things happen, rather than doing damage control after the fact. This is very important.

We Feel Guilty

If we feel guilty about making kids mind, imagine the guilt we will feel when our child gets hurt because we didn't teach him the rules of life. I heard a radio interview with a mother whose son got hit by a car. She was out on the sidewalk with her three-year-old child. He heard an ice cream truck bell and ran out into the street from between two parked cars. His mother screamed, "No!" but he ignored her, dashed out, and got hit by a car. Fortunately, the boy survived, but his mother felt terribly guilty. She said, "I had that moment to shout a warning, but in that fraction of a second, from the time I shouted and realized my son was going to ignore me, I knew I failed him as a mother. I failed to teach him discipline. I thought back on all the other times he ignored me and all I would do was repeat myself. I thought I was being caring, but I was setting the stage for disaster. All of my motherly love couldn't overcome my feelings of guilt and condemnation."

We must balance our love and discipline. Some children resent discipline and may manipulate your feelings of guilt. A child's momentary unhappiness at being made to mind is not going to leave us feeling as guilty as knowing that we let our child down by not making him mind. As this mother learned, reality can be more cruel than we will ever be.

We Don't Want to Upset the Child

Another problem is worrying that changing something in a child's life for the better will upset him or cause the child unhappiness. You may decide to seek counseling for your child's problem, or to impose more structure because your child is out of control. You may decide to make different arrangements for your child's schooling. These decisions are hard to make. If your child is deliberately not functioning in public school, he may not like home schooling because he can no longer misbehave as easily. Should we worry about how we imagine the child may feel, or whether he says he will be unhappy? Or, should we ask ourselves, "What is best for my child?"

We Don't Like to Think We Are on a Power Trip

Some of us feel guilty about setting up rules and exercising power. When we say, "I don't want my child to think that I am on a power trip," we might be saying, "I don't want to tell my child what to do because he may not love me anymore." We may also feel, "I don't want anyone telling me what to do because I am a responsible person and I hope that my child will be responsible, too (even if he obviously is not)."

We set up rules not just to exercise power. We do so because we love our children; we want to teach them how to be safe and how to grow up. The idea, "Don't interfere in their learning, let them learn on their own," is cruel when applied to dangerous situations.

We may feel, "I hate power trips and don't want to get into one with my child." If your child has a strong personality, you may already be in a power trip, whether you want to be or not. The only question is whether you win or lose. Your child may not be using physical aggression and hitting you, but if you encounter resistance every time you ask your child to do something, you are in a power struggle. Once we honestly admit this, our choices are to fulfill our responsibility as parents, or to give in to the child. Don't cave in at this point. We don't do our kids a favor by letting them walk all over us.

How Do We Get Results?

Positive and negative consequences help us reinforce and modify how our children behave. These consequences may be natural, or created by you. Some natural consequences take a long time to occur. If your child does his homework, he will get better grades, go on to college, and get a better job, but it will take years for this to happen.

Others take less time. If your child cleans up his room he will immediately be able to find things he is looking for. Some natural consequences are too harsh. If a child plays out in the street, a car could hit him. Our job as parents is to use natural consequences if they are reasonable, and when they are too slow or dangerous, we create the consequences.

If a negative consequence is needed, tell the child what it is, have the child take the consequence, and then move on. Once the child is past the consequence and is doing things properly, be sure to remind him that he is behaving like the image you want him to have of himself. Don't make the mistake of telling the misbehaving child, "That's just like you to do something stupid." Never say anything about your child that you don't want to come true. If you keep telling your child he always misbehaves, he will live up to the image you create of him.

Be a Reporter, but Slant Your Story

Imagine being a television reporter doing continuous live coverage of your child's life. By commenting on it, you provide feedback to your child. Next, assume that your child watches and hears your television report of his behavior. The slant you put on the story is going to influence your child. If you say, "Jack skipped a class at school today, which is no surprise because Jack is always misbehaving," Jack gets the message: I am always misbehaving. If we slant the story in another direction, "Jack skipped a class at school today, and that is highly unusual because Jack is always very responsible," Jack gets a very different message: I am always very responsible.

We don't overlook Jack's misbehavior. We deal with it by giving him a negative consequence and then we move on. As soon as you see yourself slanting the news in a way that portrays your child's negative behavior as normal, "That's just like Jack to hit his brother," stop and censor your report. You can't lie and say, "Jack hit his brother and that is just wonderful," and you can't say, "Jack didn't hit his brother," but after Jack gets his negative consequence for hitting his brother, reinforce the image that, "Jack treats his brother with love and respect."

There are two reasons to slant our reporting. The first is that if Jack listens to us, we want to send him the right message, rather than directing him down the wrong path ("Jack always misbehaves"). Jack will believe this about himself and it will make it easier for Jack to act as if he always misbehaves. The second reason is that if we slant the story negatively and assume that Jack always misbehaves, we begin to act as if Jack always misbehaves. Jack will pay attention to our words and actions, and act accordingly. He will live according to our expectations—good or bad. Children may have trouble living up to our highest expectations, but they seldom have trouble living down to our lowest expectations. Be careful about calling your child stupid, particularly if he outsmarts you. Tailor your reactions to encourage the good out of any behavior.

Make Sure Your Child Knows the Difference Between the Positive and Negative Consequences

It may seem strange to say that there should be a difference between praise and correction; however, the correction always should be more of a negative consequence than the praise. This seems like an obvious statement. If you recall the story of the parent whose child was hitting the dog, the parent said, "We tried explaining it to him." What this means is that the parents talked to the child. Kids learn, "If I do something wrong, my parents talk to me, and when I do something right my parents don't talk to me. I am better off doing something wrong so that my parents talk to me, even if it is a lot of stupid stuff about how I should mind."

A reward system assumes that the reward is going to be a positive experience, and that the negative consequence is a negative experience. While we as responsible citizens fear being locked up in jail, not everyone feels that way.

For example, I recently went to the lobby of our local police station to turn in something I had found in my front yard. One poor fellow was having an awful time because the receptionist kept telling him that she was sorry but they did not have any reason to arrest him. He mumbled something about having to go back to Texas to pay his debt to society. The receptionist, who was trying her best to be accommodating, said, "Well, James, I'll try checking the computer again, but so far we haven't any reason to arrest you." A few minutes later she said, "Gee, I checked with Texas again and just can't seem to find anything from the information we got back that would allow us to arrest you." For most people, jail would be a negative consequence. For this poor fellow, going to jail was more positive than the torment of his own guilt.

I spoke to a woman detective who works with young people. She was disturbed because some kids were proud of having been arrested. A supposed negative consequence has become a positive experience for these kids.

Perhaps one of the problems is that getting arrested means being handcuffed, riding to the juvenile hall in a police car, and sitting around while people ask you a bunch of questions, then your parents come and take you home. While this may be inconvenient if it happens on a weekend, it is easy to see that this could be more fun than staying in school or going to the dentist.

Of course, the most positive part of this experience is the "respect" one gets from the other kids who pride themselves on misbehaving.

Don't Rely on Rewards If They Don't Work

"My dog is biting my college housemates."

"You and your friends can attend a class together."

"I talked to them about it, but they won't do anything to discipline the dog because they only believe in positive reinforcement. The problem is that they think discipline is violence and they don't believe in violence."

"But, your dog does."

"Yes, I guess that's the problem."

You might think, "Well, my child responds to rewards. Why shouldn't I rely on them?" Certainly some children respond to rewards and positive motivators all of the time, and some respond some of the time, but not all children respond all of the time.

We want to rely on our child. Rely is the key word when we talk about training rather than teaching. Rely means to have confidence your child will do what is expected, even when the child may not feel like doing it. Why? Because that is when it really counts. That is when we may only get one chance. That is when we hope our child does what he knows he should do.

Positive reinforcement plays a large part when we teach, and we certainly use it for training, too—if it works. If it doesn't work, don't rely on it. When the positive approach doesn't work, shift to negative consequences. We all live in a world where there are positive and negative consequences. Please do not fall victim to those who insist on positive approaches only, even when the positive approach is failing miserably.

The world would be a wonderful place if everyone responded to positive motivators, but reality proves this is not true. If your youngster wants to climb through the bedroom window at night and go out with his friends more than he wants his allowance, your reward system isn't working.

If you drive a car, you stop at stop signs for one of several reasons. You don't stop at stop signs because a police officer jumps out and gives you a cookie every time you do. You stop either because you are a responsible person, or because you do not want to suffer the negative consequences of either getting hit by another car, or getting a ticket. When I walk up the stairs to my office I look to make sure I put my foot solidly on the step. If I do, I get to my office safely, if I don't, I trip and bang my shin. If I hurt my shin, I suffer physical pain, but I don't experience emotional trauma from suffering the consequences of my behavior. That's life.

The people who believe in using only positive reinforcement must feel that emotional damage will be done if the possibility of a negative consequence looms on the horizon. Reality proves otherwise. Can you recall a person having to be treated for waiting for a red light? Negative consequences could happen if we ignore the red light, but we don't go into therapy and blame all of the cars crossing in front of us on the green light; also, most of us don't blame the police for possibly being there to give us a ticket if we run the light.

Rewards may not always get your child to do something, and threatening to withhold the reward may not get your child to stop doing something. If you ask someone who believes in using only positive motivation, "But what do you do to stop a child from misbehaving?" you might be told to ignore the misbehavior, and when it stops, reward the good behavior. The problem is, that if you are supposed to wait until the bad behavior stops and the good behavior begins before giving the reward, you might wait a long time. You can't reward good behavior if it does not happen. What these positive-reinforcement-only people overlook, is the fact that for some kids and adults, misbehavior is its own reward.

Throw Down Your Gun and We'll Give You a Cookie

Suppose that someone is robbing a bank and the police arrive. They order him to surrender and he starts shooting at them with a machine gun. The police announce over a megaphone, "Throw down your gun, come out with your hands up, and we'll give you a cookie." The robber responds with more bullets. The police try another strategy, "If you don't come out, you won't get a cookie."

We laugh at the idea of the police dealing with a bank robber by offering him a cookie, or threatening not to give him one. Are we going to take seriously the same advice offered as a solution to our parenting problems? You might think, "Good grief, Harold, my child is not a bank robber," and you are right, but the principle is the same. If your child does not respond to positive reinforcement, what do you do? We as parents can look as foolish as the police offering a bank robber a cookie, when we keep offering bribes to a child who wants to misbehave more than he wants our bribes.

Imagine doing your favorite activity in life and then being asked to stop. My offer to you is that if you stop doing your favorite activity, I will allow you to do your third-favorite activity. You would laugh at me and call me a fool for expecting you to give up your favorite activity for your third-favorite activity. This only works if what you are being offered is more important to you than what you are doing. This is why positive reinforcement doesn't always work.

The Idea Sounds Good, But Rewards Alone May Not Work

"Do you use food in your dog school?"
"No."
"Good. I took my first dog to a treat training school that only used food. My dog ran across the street and got killed. I went to three sets of classes. It was a complete waste of money and I ended up losing my dog."

The greatest travesty that has hit both well-meaning dog owners and responsible parents looking for help raising children is the mistaken idea that all dogs and children will respond to positive reinforcement.

When we are tempted to use only positive reinforcement (even when it doesn't work), we actually mean well. We look for reasons to justify our actions, however inefficient they may be. Our reasons include:

1. *It is a safe way to assert ourselves—"Do it my way because I am kind and humane."*

2. *We find it emotionally satisfying to give things to others. Being the kindly distributor of goodies is fun—we get attention and thanks.*

3. *It seems kind and avoids confrontations.*

4. We can't be accused of making mistakes dealing with misbehavior because we don't do anything until something good happens.

5. We can't be blamed when what we do doesn't work. We hope our intentions are judged, rather than our results. Even if what we suggest is utter nonsense, doesn't work, and results in injury, we mean well.

6. If we make a living giving advice and our advice sounds kind, we can get people coming back even though our advice results in little, slow, or no progress.

Are we really being kind when we give a child the false impression there are no negative consequences? No, we are not. Like it or not, we live in a world with dangers, laws, other family members, friends, neighbors, and strangers with rights. As much as we love our kids, we realize that they can't always do everything they want.

I believe that the Sheltie Syndrome mentioned in chapter one is alive and well among a few psychologists and counselors who help parents with their children. They take ideas that work well with easy, cooperative kids and apply the ideas to stubborn kids, and when the kids don't respond, the parents feel like they are failures.

Of course, another problem with using rewards is that some kids will browbeat a parent for greater rewards—"I'll do my chores if you double my allowance."

I'm Sorry (I Got Caught)

Avoid thinking, "We are so glad you stopped and reformed for a minute that we will reward the slightest temporary improvement, even if it doesn't last." Another problem arises when children play the Momentary Remorse Game. In this case, a child deliberately misbehaves so he will be rewarded when he stops. Kids are smart enough to figure this out. "If I misbehave, I won't get into trouble, and then when I stop (for a while) my parents will think they have succeeded in reforming me and give me something."

Negative Consequences

If rewards don't work, we turn to negative consequences. Remember, "negative" is a relative word and can mean a lot of things. Even music can be a negative consequence. The owner of a convenience store had problems with young people loitering outside his store and bothering customers. When he installed speakers outside the store and played classical music; the loiterers left. The important thing to remember when cooking up negative consequences is that it must be negative to your child.

Time Out

One family called for a consultation about an aggressive dog that was biting their child. They had been getting help from an "animal behaviorist" who moved out of state and was no longer available to advise them. Their dog would get up on the sofa, and when the child went to move the dog it would bite him. The behaviorist had told them to tell the dog, "No," and put the dog in time out for thirty minutes.

I asked if it was working. The parent said it didn't seem to be helping, but there was some progress. I asked how long they had been doing it, the parent said, "Three years."

While this family was consistent, they didn't make much progress because they followed bad advice. It shouldn't take three years to get a dog to stop biting. Time out may temporarily stop your child's misbehavior, at least as long as the child is in time out.

The problem is that it may not be a negative consequence that prevents the misbehavior from happening again.

To counter child abuse we are told to use time out. Television ads encourage parents not to be abusive and to use time out instead of yelling and hitting kids.

Time out means removing a child from a situation and putting the child in a secluded area until he has calmed down, or has done a certain amount of penalty time. It does not mean life imprisonment, nor does it mean locking a child in his room during the teen years. It does have the advantage of preventing us from doing something violent or stupid if we are at our wit's end, but it is not a magical cure-all.

A laughable example of the misplaced trust in time out came to light recently in a newspaper report. A potential juror for Oklahoma City bomber Timothy McVeigh's trial was excused because the person didn't believe in anything more severe than time out. Even the most optimistic of us would find it hard to imagine that time out (unless it was forever) would change the behavior of a man who murdered 168 children and adults.

Boredom

I'm sure that your child has said, "I'm bored." Even before television and video games, kids got bored. If we grew up before television and had to sit through Sunday afternoons visiting adults who sat around talking with our parents for hours, we might be able to tolerate boredom a little better than our kids today. Don't overlook boredom as an effective negative consequence.

One fellow told me that when he and his wife started dating and took their first afternoon trip to the coast with her children, they were still in the saving face mode. Her children started picking on each other in the back seat. His wife did a slow burn wishing the kids wouldn't embarrass her and he just kept quiet. They were in a rural part of Oregon and radio reception was poor, but he had a self-improvement cassette in the car stereo. He turned it on thinking it would give the kids something to listen to and enjoy. The inspiring message he enjoyed listening to, at first produced silence in the back where the kids were sitting, then their slower breathing indicated that the unintentional "Boredom Bomb" had put them to sleep. From then on, any misbehavior in the car was dealt with by playing a self-improvement cassette.

Embarrassment

Embarrassment can be another useful negative consequence. When your teenager, who won't walk across the room to change a television channel, asks you to drop him off one block from school so he can get some exercise, it is obvious that you as his parent embarrass him. Whether we feel good about it or not, our teenagers are probably embarrassed by us. The first reason is simply that we are older and not "cool." The second reason is they dread the fact that we treat them like "little kids," even when they act like little kids.

After we grow up, we usually get over being embarrassed by our parents. As one friend of mine said, "Never apologize for your parents, everyone has them." However, when we are teenagers and we care about what we imagine everyone thinks about us, we are very sensitive about our parents.

You can use embarrassment as a wonderful negative consequence if your teenager starts to skip classes. You can tell him, with a straight face and a helpful smile, that you will be glad to come to school to remind him what time it is, or to help him find his classroom. See if you can work out an arrangement with the teacher to let you come in and sit in on one of your teenager's classes. Tell your teenager that the first time you come in, you will not let anyone know that you are his parent. If you have to come back a second time, the teacher will announce that you are your son's parent; if you have to come back a third time, tell your child that you will wear a beanie with a plastic propeller on it, or something equally embarrassing. Your child's teacher will be surprised that you showed up, since some parents threaten to do this, and don't. The teacher also probably will appreciate your creativity.

Most teenagers would rather walk a mile on burning coals than be embarrassed by a parent who shows up at high school wearing a beanie with a propeller on it, and a t-shirt that says, "I'm here to help Jimmy get to class on time."

Never underestimate the power of embarrassment. I just heard a news report that a city has finally come up with an incredibly effective approach to collecting unpaid traffic fines. It wasn't incarceration, or the parking boot that prevents you from driving the car. They resorted to the lowest, most diabolical trick of all, one that strikes terror in the heart of nearly every son and daughter, regardless of age. They threatened to tell the scofflaw's mother. Their recovery rate suddenly shot up to more than 80 percent.

When you use embarrassment, you might find it even more effective to be seemingly helpful. Rather than saying, "If you skip a class, I'm going to go to school and embarrass you into going to class," tell your teenager, "I know that younger children need help from their parents when they go to high school, and I will be glad to help you by coming to school to help you find your class, or remind you what time it is."

Your teenager is going to be embarrassed about your being so out of touch with reality that you think he is a younger child, needing help doing anything. He also will have nightmares about what fellow students will think when they see his parent treating him like a little kid. Teenagers can feel sympathy with others who are fighting with their parents, but will laugh at another student whose parents lovingly treat him like a nine-year-old.

While this may seem manipulative, it is a way of creating a consequence that is negative to your child.

It would be interesting to see what happens if a parent told a son, "So, you are going to join a gang. I want to go to the meetings with you to make sure that no one gives you a hard time." I wonder if the president of the gang would say, "I'd like to welcome our newest member, Bad Boy Smith and his mother, Mrs. Smith."

Be Creative and Customize Your Consequences

Unfortunately, there is no one magical, universal, negative consequence that works with all kids. Some kids respond to yelling, time out, standing in the corner, grounding, or taking away allowance, television, and contact with friends. Others don't care enough about any of these particular consequences to change their behavior. Our job as parents is to find out what works with each individual child.

I also am not promoting one particular method or technique that I think everyone should use. My idea in dog training and parenting is to use as little as will get the job done, and if that doesn't work move on to the next step. I start with a positive approach and continue until it stops working, then shift to the negative.

One way to find out what might work is to ask your child, "If you were a parent and your child did this, what would you do?" You might think, "My child is too smart to fall for that." Ask, you might be surprised at your child's response.

The other way is to watch and listen to your child. Encourage your children to talk about what they like and dislike. The more you know about your child, the more you will understand your child's likes and dislikes and be able to use this information to help him grow up to be a responsible adult. Don't feel guilty about persuading your child. Rest assured that your kid's friends will be persuasive when they talk to him about misbehaving.

Some of Us Unknowingly Reward Bad Behavior

Kids who are ignored when they behave, may learn that if something bad happens, either to them or if they misbehave, they get attention. The attention they get may seem negative because the words are about misbehavior, but getting attention can be more positive than being ignored.

Another way to reward bad behavior is to listen to it. Kids love for us to listen to them—and we should listen—but not to them bragging about stupid behavior.

When I was twelve, we visited a family with a son who had gotten in trouble shoplifting. I was cautioned not to mention it and I assumed there would be long periods of embarrassed silence as everyone avoided saying anything about his crime. After lunch, we sat down in the living room and the boy started talking about his shoplifting conviction, as I would have described a school accomplishment. I kept waiting for his parents to stop him from talking about such stupid, criminal behavior. They never did. They let him chatter on about how he had gotten away with it before, how he got caught, and the stupidity of the store security people and police. I certainly had not been perfect as a kid, but the thought of talking about my misbehavior at the dinner table in front of parents or guests was incomprehensible. What really floored me was that his parents sat there and said, "Oh, Louie, that's terrible," and then laughed an embarrassed little laugh. I wondered why they made us listen to him make such a fool of himself. Louie's stupid behavior was rewarded by our paying attention to him.

We Discourage Good Behavior

If a child does something wrong and then admits to it and is punished, he might get the idea that telling the truth doesn't pay. Care must be taken to explain that if a child does something wrong, that is one issue, and then admitting the truth, or lying, is a second issue.

We Criticize All the Time

Some of us think that being a firm parent means appearing to be strict, never smiling, and criticizing everything (even good behavior). If you were raised by a parent who always found fault, even if you were doing something right, you might act that way with your child. I experienced this when I grew up. I realized that in my mother's world, there were two options, you criticized, or you kept quiet. I never met my grandparents, but from the photos I saw, they looked like having fun was not a major part of their lives. I realized that my mother's parents must have been pretty critical of her, and it had stuck.

Don't place your child in the position of thinking that everything may be criticized. Few things are harder than doing all you can to please someone who can't be pleased. You can be firm by having rules, you can enforce them, and you can do it with a smile. Creating and using negative consequences doesn't mean you have to get angry. Just set up your rules and stick with them.

We Never Praise Good Behavior

If your parents did not criticize everything, they might have just expected you to be good and never given you any positive strokes. You may end up not praising your child's good behavior.

After you teach your child, and your child learns what to do, use positive reinforcement as long as it works. When your child fails to respond to the positive, switch to negative consequences. Take into account your child's age and find out what your child likes and doesn't like. Remember, just because something worked with you when you were a kid, or it worked with your first child, it may not work with your second, more stubborn child. Decide that you will parent longer than your child will rebel. After your child has completed the negative consequence, move on. Don't keep beating your child over the head with the mistake.

Waiting Too Long

"My dog never bit me before I started your class. What is going on?"

"It could be that you never made your dog do anything until you came to class. Dogs and kids never rebel as long as they are getting and doing everything they want."

Something like this could happen with a child who has not been disciplined. We may find the child willingly accepts that things have changed, or the child may rebel even more. We should not be surprised when this happens. A child doesn't have to push his parents around if his parents let him do whatever he wants.

It is only when we take a stand and set up rules that a child who has been allowed to get away with everything takes exception to our setting limits.

What happens when we let a child grow up without any discipline, and then decide we are going to step in and do our job as parents? My experience with dogs is that one of two things happens. Either the dog improves immediately, or, if the dog has had a lot of experience backing his owners down, the dog rebels even more.

Facing the thought of our children rebelling against us, we might feel that it is too late to change a child's attitude. Parenting isn't always easy and in spite of our best efforts, our kids might do stupid and dangerous things. My approach has been to strive for perfection, accept that it is never going to happen, and most importantly, deal with the imperfection that life throws at me.

Stay a Step Ahead

"Our pup's breeder said not to take our dog to training class because this breed is too intelligent to be trained."

We laugh at the idea of someone breeding a dog so intelligent than the breeder can't train the dog. While both dogs and kids do outsmart us on occasion, we should be able to keep one step ahead of them.

Fortunately, there are many excellent books about childhood development through which we can learn what to expect from our children. Resources focusing on children can reassure us that our child (though not perfect) is within a normal range, or alert us to problems that require professional help.

By all means, learn as much as you can about your child, but please don't stop there. Learning how to manage your child is half of your job. The other half is learning how to manage yourself and to become as highly skilled at parenting as you can. This book is not about children as much as it is about how we guide, nurture, and respond to our children. When I first thought about becoming a parent, I thought, "No way, I don't know what I am doing." I stopped for a moment and thought that several of the things I now do very well were things that I knew nothing about when I started them. I learned how to train dogs, teach dog training classes as a business, and enjoy SCUBA diving as a hobby.

When I first opened my dog training school, I thought I would be working with dogs. After a year, I noticed that the dogs never called up and they never came by to enroll for training. They always came in with people. While I obviously had to learn how to train dogs to open my business, I discovered that the key to my success at teaching people how to train their dogs was to improve my people skills. Just as dog training involves both the dogs and the dog owners, parenting includes not only learning about children but also learning how we guide and react to our kids.

When I decided to marry a woman with children, I considered it another "How To" project. In this book, I have shared with you the ideas that helped me. I don't claim to have all the answers you will need, but I sincerely hope that this book has given you the idea that parenting is not just doing what comes naturally. Approach parenting just as you do your job or any other activity. It is a series of learnable, intellectual, and emotional skills. Learn how to do what you need to do and stick with it.

When your family life is going smoothly, parenting can be wonderfully rewarding. When difficulties arise, it can be the most frustrating experience you will ever encounter. You can always quit your job, but you can't fire your kids. While parenting can be difficult, it helps to think of it as a game in which your job is to stay a step ahead of your child. If your child outsmarts you, learn your lesson and be prepared for the next time. Mistakes happen and it pays to be kind to your children and yourself. Parent with a smile and above all, do it with love.

Some of my dog training students say, "I know I am the problem." I like to assure them (and the same is true of you as a parent), "You are not the problem, you are the solution to the problem."

✔ After we teach our kids what to do, we move on to training to bring out natural abilities.

✔ Training makes sure the child does what he knows he should do.

✔ Both teaching and training are important.

✔ Feeling guilty won't give your child the tools he needs to succeed as an adult.

✔ Don't worry about upsetting your child—reality will be much harsher that a loving parent will be.

✔ You don't have to be on a power trip to teach or train your children.

✔ What are the things you've done that get results? Apply those methods to other situations.

✔ Deal with an issue and then move on.

✔ Be a reporter, but slant your story so as to encourage your child to learn.

✔ Make sure your child knows the difference between right and wrong.

✔ Are the positives positive, and the negatives negative to the child?

✔ Don't rely on rewards if they don't work.

✔ Consequences should be appropriate and timely.

✔ Negative consequences can be very powerful motivators.

Appendixes

The following sections are helpful for those of you with dogs and children. While they are more focused on dog behavior, you will find many of the lessons already mentioned embedded in these sections. These are some of the lessons that helped me choose dog training as my model for developing this dog training comparison to parenting.

Appendix A

Parents, Not Vendors

Parents as Vending Machines

As you watch parents interact with their children, see if you can pick out the parents who act like vending machines. Notice the momentary satisfaction the child expresses when he gets something and then notice the drastic change when the parent stops vending.

The parent may stop vending because the parent ran out of what the child wants, or the parent stops vending because the parent just decides that enough is enough. You will see the same reaction one would have to an empty vending machine, or worse, one that took your money and didn't deliver.

Why You Should Not Rely On Rewards

This section relates not only to dogs but also to the parenting philosophy that focuses on only using rewards and positive reinforcement. While positive reinforcement is one element of good dog training and parenting, the simple fact is that it doesn't always work when dogs and children find misbehaving more fun than the positive reinforcement you offer.

Just recently, I had a call from someone whose dog was very aggressive. She explained that she didn't feel that her current trainer was giving her much help. When I asked what was happening, she said that her dog stood on one side of the fence trying to attack a dog on the other side. She said, "I can't believe this, the trainer is standing next to my dog waving a sausage at him, trying to distract him as he bites the fence."

Dog Knows, But Won't Do It

Owners complain, "My dog knows what to do, and he will do it for food, but he won't do it for me." You might think, "I have used food to teach my dog before, why shouldn't I rely on it?"

You will admit that there is a big difference between your dog knowing something and doing it only when he wants to, and your dog doing things the first time you tell him even when there is a big distraction.

I know that dogs can be taught some things if you use food for a reward. If all you want to do is "Show Dog Training" or to teach your dog a few tricks like "roll over" or "begging" you might find food reward training to be the way to go. But, most of us want more than that for our dog.

What Is Wrong With Relying on Food Training?

The answer is pretty simple. If your dog wants to chase a cat across the street *more than* your dog wants food, you are sunk.

Imagine that you have just finished a large delicious meal at home or at your favorite restaurant. As you get up from the table someone asks you to do something you don't really want to do. When they say they will give you a cookie for doing this thing you don't want to do, you refuse. You feel like you couldn't eat anything else. Food would not be a very good reward and it would not get you to do what you don't want to do.

I talked to an old-time dog trainer who said that he would get a dog in for training and hold food back from the dog for seventy-two hours. "Then the food meant something to the dog," he explained. I understood his point. I figured that if I had been starved for three days, food would mean a lot to me.

I'm sure that you will agree that holding food back for that long is something you wouldn't feel comfortable doing. I know that I wouldn't. It also means that you can only train the dog every three days.

The fact is that there are things that dogs like to do more than eating. For some dogs chasing, hunting, fighting, guarding, protecting or extending territory, curiosity, sex, fear, and aggression might be stronger motivators than food. If you accept this fact, you cannot rely on food to help you train your dog to mind you around powerful distractions.

There is a widely accepted principle in psychology that we have basic needs that are very important. Once these needs are met, we simply take them for granted. I SCUBA dive and air is very important when I am ninety feet underwater. Air is obviously important when I am walking around on land too, but if you approach me on the street and say, "Harold, you can breathe all of the air you want today for only one dollar," I would laugh at you for making a ridiculous offer. On the other hand, if I were to have problems with my SCUBA tank while I was underwater, I would pay you anything you asked for enough air to get me back to the surface.

Can Food Training Stop Bad Behavior?

Food training often is used by people who believe that dogs can be trained by using only praise and positive reinforcement. One couple came to my class with a dog that was chasing and trying to bite the girl next door. The man only believed in positive reinforcement. After he tried positive reinforcement to stop his dog from biting the girl next door and failed, he came to class. He attended the first class and never returned. His wife called and said he simply would not give up his belief in positive reinforcement as a cure, even when it obviously didn't work with his own dog.

Several months later, his wife came by to purchase a leash. I asked how the dog was doing. Her answer was that while their dog was still trying to chase and bite her, the girl "was growing up." I guess that the idea was that eventually the girl would grow up and leave the neighborhood.

The problem with food reward and using only positive reinforcement is that it is very difficult to stop unwanted behavior. I would have bet that this family could have built a wall of hot dogs or some other treat between their house and that of the girl next door and their dog would eat just enough of the hot dogs so that he could get to his target on the other side.

Dogs do things like chase, fight, and bite which can cause injury. Does this mean that food training should be used with all dogs, except those with serious problems? No, because even a friendly dog running across the street to play with another dog can be hurt or killed by a car. Any time you want to be able to *rely* on your dog doing something, do not use food training.

Why Do People Use Food for Training?

First, some people like feeding their dogs and getting the attention a dog will pay them when they have food, just as parents like the attention they get from their children when they dole out presents. Second, it seems like the "kind" way to train a dog for people who feel guilty about wanting to make their dog do things the dog may not want to do. Some people actually believe, "Who are we, as people, to make our dogs do what they don't want to do?" Unfortunately, these dogs seldom have any freedom because the owners can't trust them off the leash. There is a school of "Progressive Trainers" who advocate "Inducement Training" and criticize "Compulsion Training." While "compulsion" sounds terribly mean, their definition includes anything that actually has the trainer "physically make" the dog do anything. The difference between an "Induced" and "Compulsive" sit would be that if you even gently placed the dog in the sit position, it is considered "Compulsive." They believe that you should hold a treat above the dog's head long enough so that the dog's neck will get tired and he will eventually sit for the treat.

Are we really being kind when we do something that could not only let us down, but that could cost our dog his life? I don't feel that we are being kind by doing this. Like it or not, we live in a world with traffic dangers, dog control laws, neighbors with rights, and friends and relatives who don't want to be jumped on, chased, or bitten. As much as we love our dogs, we realize that they can't always do everything they want.

What are Some of the Other Problems With Using Food?

Your dog can learn the wrong lessons when being trained with food. A woman called and said that she had started giving her little Shih Tzu treats whenever she came in from the backyard. She started laughing and said that now her dog asks to go out in the backyard so that she can come back in and get a treat. She added, "And she gets me up at three in the morning to do this."

Fred Growls at the Vending Machine

Dear Joan:

When you left class early, I wondered whether or not you would come back. Several weeks have gone by and I have missed seeing you. I am really sorry that it appears that you will not be returning with your dog, Fred.

You first started Fred in class when he was four months old. You were smart for doing that because his breed gets very large, very powerful and is inclined to challenge the people who try to make them mind. When you came back with him this time, he was about eight months old. This is the dog's teenage time when you would expect your dog to rebel and test you.

Usually when someone comes back, it is easier the second time. It seemed hard for you because you have one of the most challenging dogs in the class. In his case, he seemed to attract more attention than the other dogs because he was still growling at dogs in the fourth week and he was growling at you. His growling also attracted my attention and I would stop the class and give you suggestions. It must have been uncomfortable for you to have him growling and then having me single you out.

You came to the second week of this class with a different training collar than I recommend. When I suggested that you would find it easier working Fred with the collar I use, you mentioned that you were taking him to another class where they use the other collar. I wondered about your decision to take two different classes, but dismissed it, figuring that you have the right to attend as many different classes as you wish.

The collar you were using should have tipped me off as to why Fred was growling at you because the other class uses a thinner collar and also uses treats for training.

I remember that you left with Fred in the middle of a class when he was growling at you and I was helping you. I'm not sure if you were embarrassed by Fred's behavior or whether you were tired of me encouraging you to get him to stop growling at you.

The week after you left, a student called me with a question about her dog. She said that she had seen you giving Fred treats. She missed the first class and wondered if I had told students to use treats. I told her that we didn't use treats. She said she noticed that you only gave treats while I was looking the other way.

When she mentioned the treats and I remembered your comment about the thin collar, I suddenly realized why Fred was growling at you for what seemed to be no apparent reason. Most dogs challenge their owners when the people make the dog do something the dog does not what to do. While I was looking the other way, I would hear him growl and turn around and see you standing there while he was sitting at an angle facing you. You did not appear to be making him do anything and I could not figure out why he was growling at you. I now believe that he was growling at you because he was mad at you for not giving him another treat.

I am sure that you have seen people put money into a vending machine and then end up losing their coins. People yell at the machines, slam the machines with their hands, and even kick them. In fact, people have gotten killed because they started banging on the machines to such a degree that the machines fell over on top of them.

There are many ways people have described the relationship between a pet owner and a pet. Some think of themselves as leader of the pack and the pet as a member of the pack.

Some are honest enough to admit that those roles are reversed. Others think of their pets as members of their family. I often suspect that my cat Walter thinks that I am a food vendor. Your dog seems to treat you like a vending machine. You might have problems with your dog if you are using the ideas that your other instructor teaches and then use the ideas I teach.

Joan, you are a very strong woman. I find it interesting that you wear a button stating your position about one of the most controversial issues in our country today. It is an issue where you are either on one side or the other and there seems to be no room for compromise. I am sure that you wear this button because you have very strong convictions and you are brave enough to state your position. I'd bet that by wearing this button you are exposing yourself and your strongly held beliefs to the criticism of the people on the other side of this issue. What puzzles me is that while you are very strong when it comes to some of your personal beliefs, you don't seem to want to get your dog to accept you as being in charge.

What I am concerned about is that unless you clearly convince Fred that you are in charge, he will gladly assume the position of power. Neither dogs nor children respect a vending machine. They will use the vending machine as long as it provides them what they want, when they want it. When it stops vending, it is treated with scorn.

If you continue to let this happen with Fred, you are going to be living with a time bomb. You will be forcing yourself to impose a number of rules on yourself and the others Fred has contact with. You will find yourself living your life dictated by what your dog Fred likes and doesn't like.

Please abandon your role as a vending machine. Both you and Fred will be happier.

Other Complaints about Food Training

People who use food to train their dog have to carry food with them. One woman called and said, "I'm tired of running around with these stupid frankfurters in my pockets."

Another woman called and said that she was annoyed because she would have to stop and wait for her dog to eat the treat.

One man said, "If my dog does it right, I give him a treat, but what do I do when he is doing something wrong? If I give him a treat, he will continue to misbehave, and not giving him a treat isn't going to stop him from misbehaving."

One woman said, "I get so darned mad about this food thing, it's like he will only mind when I bribe him. I feel stupid having that kind of relationship with my dog."

Finally, one woman said, "The trouble with food training is that it just doesn't last."

Using food training can also be a problem when you waste your time and effort using food to coax your dog to do something, and then when it counts, your training fails.

When I left high school teaching in 1976 to open my dog school, I wanted to open a dog school for people who wanted more than just "Show Dog Training," a place where they could get help with common problems. I looked into different training techniques and picked what I felt was the best. I care too much for my dogs to rely on food training and I would never use it with those clients who trust me to teach them how to have a dog they can rely on.

Training and Teaching Consistently

There are many approaches to dog training and parenting. Some of us believe that we should take a little bit of this and a little bit of that and mix it all together and come up with something that works. At some superficial levels this may work, but I suggest that your basic approach to dog training and parenting remain consistent.

As parents, we might be tempted to bounce back and forth. Please understand that switching from "positive" to "negative" consequences in a system that regularly uses both is being consistent. Switching from using "positive only" to "positive and negative" is *not* being consistent.

The Dangers of Mixing and Matching

I was tempted twice to mix and match. One is described in Appendix D when I unsuccessfully used the Alpha Roll and got bitten. My approach is based on the idea that the person is responsible for teaching the dog to adapt to our people world. It is very structured and I believe a very fair balance of positive and negative (when the positive fails) consequences. The person decides what is acceptable behavior for the dog and the dog follows the guidance.

I was helping a very large dog that was not very confident. The person who owned the dog also was not very confident and I let this influence my approach. The owner asked if I would try an approach that she had read in a book. Instead of my normal structured approach, I read the section in the book she mentioned and it sounded like it had a solution to the dog's problem of not walking on a leash. The approach was just about the opposite of what I would usually do. It involved me getting down on the floor at the dog's level and waiting for the dog to move. As I sat on the floor near the dog, I could sense the dog's discomfort and I realized that the dog hadn't read the book and didn't have any idea of what I was doing. I thought of the idea of giving a monkey a typewriter and that eventually the monkey, just by striking random keys, would write a great book. After several uncomfortable minutes, I stood up and broke off the training session.

Switching from a technique that involved me setting things up and the dog responding, to me sitting with dog and waiting for the dog to figure things out just didn't make sense.

Parenting — A Constant Role

I taught at Thurston High School before I opened my dog training school. We as community members were horrified last year by the actions of a student who had been caught with a gun at school. He was arrested and released to his father's custody. They went home and the boy shot and killed his father and later his mother. The next day, he went to school, killed two students, and injured many more. Obviously, there was a lot of press, and some comments were made that blamed the parents.

I had only known the father as a fellow teacher in school and did not know his family. I gave some thought to the criticism that he had switched his approach from being a "pal" to being a "boss." I don't know how true the characterization of the man was, but I wondered if the switch wasn't appropriate for what the son was doing. If you are playing with your child, you can be a pal, while, if you are dealing with your son's illegal behavior, you are going to have to take a stronger authority position.

As parents, we wear many hats: teacher, judge, police officer, counselor, and supporter. I believe that we can switch from role to role as we find it appropriate. Where we do run into problems is when we change how we fulfill each role. If your child forgets to brush his teeth, you will not deal with it as severely as if he hits his sister. What is important is that we are consistent with what happens each time that your child forgets to brush his teeth and what happens each time that he hits his sister.

You can and must play different roles as a parent. The important thing is to be consistent within each role.

Appendix B

Is He "Dumb" or Is He Outsmarting You?

One of the interesting habits we have is calling our dogs and our kids "dumb." What's funny about our calling someone "dumb" is when we do it. As you begin this chapter, answer these questions.

1. Do you call your dog or child "dumb" or "stupid"?

2. Do you think your dog or child is untrainable or beyond hope?

3. Do you say these things after your dog or child has done something you consider "wrong"?

4. Do you ever get the idea that your dog or child has out-smarted you?

5. Have you ever jokingly said that your dog or child is smarter than you are?

When people ask me which are the most intelligent breeds, we must define intelligence. Our first definition is usually, "A dog that does what we want it to do." With our children we might also define intelligence as a child who minds us. Some breeds of dogs are very intelligent but they are not necessarily cooperative. Both the Siberian Huskies and the Alaskan Malamutes are considered very intelligent when it comes to learning how to open the gate in the backyard and run away. They are intelligent, but not always cooperative about staying close to home.

We often are puzzled when intelligent people commit outrageous crimes. We mistakenly assume that because someone is intelligent, they are responsible.

Some children are more intelligent that others and some may be so intelligent that they manipulate us or fool us and we are tempted to call them dumb. From this dog example, we will see that what we call dumb may not be dumb at all.

> I had a booth at the county fair one summer. People would stop by and pet my dog or ask questions about how to train dogs. One afternoon, my dog fell asleep and one fellow looked at him, looked up at my "Heeling Free Dog School" sign and asked, "Is he dead?" He had gotten "Heeling" and "Healing" confused.
>
> A while later, another man walked by and laughed at my booth. He said, "You couldn't do anything with my dog. He is too dumb."
>
> I asked, "Why do you think your dog is too dumb?"
>
> He said, "Oh, he does anything he wants."
>
> I smiled as the person walked away and I thought that his dog sure didn't sound too dumb to me. Any dog or child who can do anything he wants is certainly not dumb. Whenever

*someone says this, I suspect that the dog or the child is out-
smarting the owner or parent.*

*I have also had students in my dog classes say, "I think my
dog may be smarter than I am." I reassure my students that
there is a difference between being outsmarted occasionally and
having a dog that is actually smarter than the person. I also tell
them that dogs do outsmart their owners and that it even happens to me once in a while. I also like to reassure the person
that the dog won't be able to outsmart the two of us together.*

What can you do to be sure that your dog or your child is not
outsmarting you? When he is doing something that you might call
dumb, ask yourself the following questions:

1. What do I want him to do?

2. What is he doing now?

3. Does he understand what is expected or is he confused
   because I have failed to teach him what to do?

To understand this point, imagine being in a country where you
do not speak the language. You decide to go jogging before break-
fast. As you walk out of the hotel to start running, a man standing
out in front points at you and begins shouting at you over and over.
You don't know what the words mean, but the person looks angry
and you figure he is probably calling you a name. As you continue
your run, you hope that this loudmouth won't be there when you
return. To make your day even worse, five blocks from the hotel,
three men grab you and take your money and your watch. When
you return from your run, the man starts shouting at you again. You

run past him into the lobby of the hotel, approach the English-speaking desk clerk and mention that you were robbed and that there is a man out front yelling at you. The desk clerk says, "You must have headed east when you left the hotel." You say yes and ask him how he knows and what that has to do with the man yelling at you. The desk clerk explains that the man out front is a security guard and he was trying to warn you not to go east because many tourists are robbed when they travel in that direction. If we could understand the man advising us and we ignored his advice, we would be doing something dumb. However, we didn't understand him and could not take his advice.

Let's look at an example that applies to both dogs and children that will help you understand these three points.

First, what do I want him to do? Suppose that you want your dog or your child to come back to you when you call him using the word "come." That is your goal.

Second, what is he doing now? Instead of coming to you, he runs away, or he stops and looks at you, but doesn't come to you. With children, we also may experience an argument. "But my friend is playing outside and you told me I could play outside this morning." Or, "Mommy said that I could play outside."

Third, does he understand the situation? He may not understand what he is supposed to do, or he may think that when you call, he can come back if he wants to, or he may know what to do, and just ignore you.

The important point is that when you are teaching your dog or your child, make sure that you know what you are doing. As obvious as this statement may be, some of us act before we think and we hold a child responsible for something he doesn't understand.

Is he misbehaving intentionally? Could it be that you just haven't taught him what to do when he hears the word "come?"

Could it be that you haven't taught anything, and you just expect him to know what you want?

Many people call me with their dog problems and say, "He knows what he is supposed to do, but he just won't do it."

There are also people who like to pretend that this just could not be true. These people actually believe that dogs and kids always want to please. They are like the people who stood under apple trees disputing Isaac Newton's Law of Gravity while apples fell on their heads.

When I hear this, I think of the calls I have gotten from people who have a dog that has just bitten a child on the face, or killed the family cat, or been run over. I wonder how these people would feel if I told them that their "dogs always want to please."

The real tragedy is that people read some of these "always want to please" books or come in contact with people who believe this and take their advice. Imagine a parent of a child reading a book or talking to a child therapist who said, "You should never discipline a child for anything, but if he gets too naughty, kill him."

Can you imagine anyone sane acting on this advice? Believe it or not, there are dog books written that deliver this kind of advice about dogs. For now, let's assume that you accept the fact that some dogs and kids don't want to please and are happy outsmarting us.

While some dogs know what to do and choose not to do it, others may not fully understand what you expect them to do. One of the funniest examples of this was a very smart dog in one of my classes twelve years ago. There are four breeds that I believe tend to think ahead of their owners. I'm sure there are more, but the four I see consistently thinking ahead are the Shetland Sheepdog, Border Collie, American Eskimo, and the Keeshond. I am not saying they are always doing what they are supposed to, but I do believe they are often a step ahead of their owners.

In this class, I saw a dog walking along next to her owner. The owner stopped and the dog stopped and sat like she was supposed to and then looked up at the person. There was no response from the person and the dog laid down and then looked up again. There was still no feedback from the owner. Finally, the dog stood up and looked at the owner. All that the dog saw was the man standing there scratching his head. If the dog could talk, she probably would have said, "What do you want me to do? I tried all three positions."

I am sure that you have seen children do their best to please their parents, but the parents fail to give the child any feedback. The child may think, "It doesn't matter what I do, my parents don't care." Parents also may give neutral feedback such as, "I am busy now," and their children regard this as rejection. You may indeed be busy and it is wise to respond in a way that lets your child know that you are not just ignoring him. You can communicate that you are happy that your child is doing something useful and you will be glad to acknowledge his effort as soon as you are finished. This can be a fine line to draw, on the one hand you don't want to give your child the power to interrupt you whenever he wants to, and you also don't want to overlook your chance to acknowledge your child's efforts to do what is right.

Appendix C

The "Unexpected" Dog Bite

Of all the problems my clients call about, the most serious and the most preventable one is biting. This information is included to help you prevent your child from getting bitten.

Fortunately, most dogs give warnings weeks or months in advance that they are going to bite "unexpectedly." Learning to spot these warning signs and discovering why the family dog bites will alert you and help you prevent your child from getting hurt.

Simply getting rid of the dog may solve the immediate problem, but without learning the warning signs and finding out why the dog bit, your family may relive the same experience with its next dog.

Warning Signs

1. Growling and nipping at children are obvious actions that we sometimes overlook or dismiss with comments like, "The dog is a little rough with the kids and snaps at them, but it's just in play," or, "He's left red marks before, but he has never broken the skin, until this time." One dog owner said, "Oh no, he's never shown any signs of biting," and minutes later changed the statement to, "He's never drawn blood before."

If we see a child swinging an arm at another child, we recognize it as hitting, whether it causes injury to the victim or not. Apply the same standard to your dog. It is easier to overlook something troublesome than to recognize it as a problem and then deal with it. Be alert to these play bites, near misses, and "it didn't break the skin" bites. One of two things happens with a dog that is giving these warnings. You either recognize these signs as biting and stop it or it gets worse.

2. Of even greater concern is the dog biting, growling at, or threatening an adult in the family. A dog that is permitted (or playfully incited) to do this will have very little respect for the children in the family.

3. Is the dog chasing dogs, cats, squirrels, or other furry critters off your property? Aggression toward other animals is a definite danger signal when you have small children. Dogs that are normally friendly and obedient with adults, but quarrelsome with other dogs or cats, often treat younger children as if they were another animal.

4. Is the dog bossy toward the children? This includes pushing or bumping the kids, guarding a toy or food, or not allowing the children to do certain things. Multiply your concern by five if the dog does this to adults in your family.

5. Is the dog shy, fearful, or unpredictable around the children? While aggressive breeds can be dangerous, they also seem to let you know earlier that you should avoid them. A dog that growls or looks at you with a hard stare thirty feet away is telling you to leave him alone.

Shy and unpredictable dogs may not give you a warning until you are within their defensive zone. As a parent and a dog trainer, I am just as concerned about my family's safety when we see a fearful, unpredictable dog as when we encounter an obviously aggressive dog. Be careful of the dog that has a wide-eyed fearful look.

Teach your children that a shy or fearful dog can be dangerous because we may feel sorry for it. When we try to rescue the dog, we may cause it to feel trapped and threatened, and we may trigger the dog's defensive mechanism.

6. Is the dog tense around the children? Trying to read a dog's body language can be confusing. If your dog acts tense when your child is present, call a reliable trainer for help.

Concerns about the Neighbor's Dog

Along with the danger signs that apply to your family dog, there are several other cautions that should be observed with other dogs that your child will encounter.

1. Does a dog have to be locked up or kept away from people when company comes? While this is an attempt to solve a problem, it also alerts us to be more cautious about letting our child visit a friend with a dog that must be locked away.

An obvious concern is whether there will be an adult present to be sure that the children do not mistakenly expose themselves to danger by releasing the dog.

2. Dog owners who tie a dog up because they do not have a fence are doing their best to keep their dog away from others. The problem is that tying a dog up does not keep children away from the dog. A dog that is tied and has no path of escape may bite defensively if it feels threatened.

3. Watch for dogs that growl and are then mistakenly petted by the owner in an effort to calm the dog.

4. Dogs that are walked on a tight leash can be more danger-ous than dogs that are trained to walk on a loose leash.

Never allow your child to pet a dog if the owner has the dog pulled up next to him on a short, tight leash because of the poten-tial danger. Being held on a tight leash gives the dog the feeling that he is trapped and cannot avoid the threat your child may seem to pose.

The tight leash also communicates the dog owner's worry to the dog. While the dog owner is worrying, "I hope that my dog doesn't bite this parent and child," the dog may think, "My owner is worried. I better protect her from the threat this parent and child pose."

5. Teach your child to respect all dogs, not just the breeds that were bred to be aggressive. A little bit of information can be dan-gerous if we mistakenly think that a dog will not bite because the breed is supposed to be friendly. In the course of two days, I had that lesson driven home to me. A family lived next to a park and had a Doberman Pinscher. People from the park would climb the family's fence and use their hot tub at night. The family asked me to evaluate the dog for possible protection training but the dog was not suited at all. The next day I visited another family with one of the friendliest and least aggressive breeds, a Basset Hound. As soon as I entered their home, the dog tried to viscously attack me. Teaching children that some breeds can be more dangerous is smart, but do not make the mistake of teaching your child that any breed is totally safe.

6. Teach your child to leave strange dogs alone. This includes dogs that are alone or with a stranger. Remember that criminals sometimes use dog or lost puppy stories to lure children.

7. If a trusted neighbor's dog is on the leash and seems calm and your child is with you, teach your child to approach the dog and owner from the front.

8. Teach your child to ask permission. If the dog owner says "No," explain to your child that it is nothing personal toward your child. The dog owner may know that the dog is not good with children.

Why Dogs Become Biters

Knowing what your dog was bred to do will give you some idea of the dog's tendency to be aggressive.

Dogs bred to guard, fight, use their mouth aggressively, or to chase and kill other animals are usually more aggressive than other breeds. While you can train dogs to overcome these tendencies, it does help to learn about the breed before you get it.

Special Warning

Do not rely on what the breed of dog is "supposed" to be like when you do see evidence of biting. Regardless of your dog's breed, if you see any of the danger signs, get help.

Common Mistakes

Most dogs that bite do so because we have done one or more of the following activities.

- Rough play or wrestling.

- Tug of war—This teaches the dog that it is acceptable to bite at the end of a person's arm. When the sock or tug toy is not there to bite, the dog may go for the hand.

- Chase games—Chasing a ball is a popular game that teaches the dog to run after something that is moving and bite at it. An owner of a dog that chased children complained, "The trouble is that the kids move."

Some dog owners think that not playing chase the ball means the dog won't get any exercise. The good news is that playing fetch is fine. The difference between chasing and fetching is that with fetching, you hold the dog back until the object stops moving before releasing the dog to retrieve it.

- Encouraging play biting—Putting on a pair of heavy leather gloves and teaching the dog to bite us makes it hard for the dog to know the difference between right and wrong.

It's better (and easier) to teach the dog, "Do not bite," rather than, "You can bite me when I have welding gloves on, but don't bite my child, or anyone who will sue us."

- Failing to set up any rules for the dog—When a dog with a strong will is placed in a situation without any rules or structure, the dog will attempt to become the one in charge. This dog may become aggressive to assume or keep the leadership position.

A fearful or submissive dog finding itself in a situation without rules may resort to defensive panic, and bite unexpectedly.

Imagine a group of people in an emergency. If a strong-willed leader is present, she will begin to establish a structure. If no one has the confidence to be the leader, the group is likely to resort to panic.

People with shy or fearful dogs tend to be afraid to train them because they fear that the dog will be overwhelmed. The opposite is true, shy dogs desperately need structure to feel safe and secure.

The following also are mistakes:

• Unintentional praise of aggressive behavior—Remember, "What you pet is what you get." Stroking the dog when it is barking and trying to bite tells the dog, "I am happy that you are acting aggressively."

• Praising the dog by stroking it when the dog is fearful— If your dog is shy or fearful, call a reliable trainer for help.

• Picking up the dog—Is the dog expected to tolerate being picked up, hugged, or sat on? Some dogs feel trapped if hugged, or are afraid of falling if picked up.

Picking a dog up elevates the dog to the same level as the parent or child. It also places the dog's face near the person's, increasing the chance of a face bite.

• Playing at the dog's level—When the dog is sufficiently trained to be reliable, this can be done, but if the dog is aggressive, encourage children to stay up and out of range.

• Trying many different training methods that don't work— Each time an owner uses a training technique that doesn't work, the dog learns to resist. Should a child attempt to discipline a dog that resists the efforts of an adult, the child could get bitten.

• Experiencing a mini guard-dog-training course with someone who makes deliveries—This involves the dog learning to drive off someone like the mail carrier by the daily repetition of the following: the mail carrier approaches, the dog barks, the mail is delivered, and the mail carrier leaves. As this sequence repeats, the dog thinks, "Someone comes, I act aggressively, and the person leaves." What may be a slight "woof" in the beginning may develop into snarling and snapping as the dog learns that aggression drives the unwelcome intruder away. When visitors are let in the door, the dog may try to bite.

Offensive or Defensive Bites

Offensive bites are those where the dog makes the move toward the child. The child walks or runs past the dog and the dog goes after the child. Defensive bites happen when the child touches a sleeping dog, picks the dog up, hugs the dog, gets down on the floor with the dog, corners the dog, or in any other way invades the dog's defensive zone.

Offensive biting initiated by the dog seems to be more serious because we feel, "How dare our dog go after our child?" Actually, from a training standpoint, it is easier to work with offensive biters because the dog only needs to be taught not to go after the child. When the bite is defensive, the dog must be trained to leave the child alone and the child must be taught to leave the dog alone.

Could It Happen Again?

You will either stop the dog from biting or the problem will get worse. It usually takes time for a dog to reach the point of biting, but once the dog steps over the line, another bite may happen soon, unless the dog is taught to stop biting completely.

Trusting Your Child With Your Dog

Our attitudes toward our child and dog may need to be reevaluated. I spoke with a parent whose dog was showing signs of aggression toward her five-year-old son whom she described as "hyperactive."

Her dog-training goal was to have the dog tolerate her son's unpredictable behavior and to be able to trust the dog around her two-year-old daughter.

While I firmly believe that dogs should be held accountable for their behavior, I also know that any dog pushed into a defensive position might bite.

I asked whether she would leave her daughter alone with her son. Without hesitation she said, "No, I wouldn't." If a parent can't trust a child with other family members, the unpredictable child certainly should not be trusted with the family pet. Aggressive children may provoke dogs into equally aggressive behavior.

Dogs should not be left alone with a child under eight years old. There are *no* exceptions. Dogs usually don't think of younger children as people but as other dogs.

One family I am working with has a dog that is having trouble getting along with the daughter. The dog had been recovering from surgery (she had been spayed and had her rear dew claws removed). The mother and I had set up some guidelines to protect her daughter. When the mother called and said that the dog had nipped at her daughter again, I asked how it happened. The mother told me that she took a nap and instructed her daughter to "keep an eye on the dog." This was supposed to mean that the daughter would observe the dog and wake her mother if needed.

What happened was that the daughter approached the dog to "take a closer look" at the dog and the dog bit her.

The Family Dog as a Teacher

Along with companionship, a dog can provide for our children—we can also think of having a dog at home as a way to teach our children how they should act with other dogs. One father told me they had a lovable black and white Cocker Spaniel and that his son thought all black and white dogs were friendly. Your child will learn how to deal with other dogs from the way you teach your child to act with your dog.

The good news is that by learning the danger signals, you will be able to spot the warnings that most dogs give for weeks or months before they bite. If you see any of these warning signs with your dog, call a reliable trainer for help. Don't delay. Protect your family and your dog from the heartbreak that a dog bite can cause. Your children and your dog depend on you. Early intervention can change your dog's behavior and protect your child.

Should You Involve Your Child in Rehabilitating a Biter?

As much as we as parents want to involve our children in life lessons, working with a biter is not the job we should assign our child. We teach children to be kind to animals and then, when it comes time to turn the biting dog away from that behavior, we expect a child to be firm. Think of it as, "You bake the cake and your child gets to eat it," rather than having your child in the kitchen with you while you are baking the cake.

Find a trainer who knows how to deal with biters and start working with basic commands like sit. When your dog is trained to the point where the dog will sit ten out of ten times the first time you say the command, then you can have your child join you and tell the dog to sit. If the dog responds, have your child praise the dog, but if the dog does not respond, you as the adult should follow through and make the dog sit. Do not expect the child to be able to follow through with the same degree of confidence and competence that you have. When your dog has mastered this sitting exercise, you can have the dog lie down instead. But save the lying down exercise until last—it is the hardest and requires the most skill and determination to accomplish.

Appendix D

Becoming the Alpha Dog Without Using the Alpha Roll

As parents, we have to observe behavior and make decisions based on what we think we have seen. Jumping to a false conclusion because we misunderstand what we see can cause us to deal with a child's behavior in the wrong way. The following discusses the second dumbest dog training idea I have ever encountered. It is called the Alpha Roll.

Warning: This section describes a dog training technique that can be very dangerous. Part of the danger is that, unfortunately, this technique works some of the time, giving the people who recommend it the false sense that the average dog owner should use it with aggressive dogs. When it doesn't work, you can be injured. The first (and last) time I did it, the dog bit my hands six times. I have heard of other people who suffered severe bites on the face.

I include this information for two reasons, one is for your safety, and the other is to help you develop your ability to see things for what they really are, rather than what they appear to be. As we shall discover, this dog training technique is based on a misinterpretation of what we see dogs doing.

What Is It Supposed to Accomplish?

The Alpha Roll is supposed to help you get your dog to stop biting you and to convince the dog that you are the leader of the pack.

Some of us mistakenly think that just being nice to the family dog is a substitute for training. We are terribly disappointed when our dog starts getting aggressive with our family. If we let the family dog drift along without any guidance, then when the dog's misbehavior becomes intolerable and dangerous, we may decide to have the dog destroyed.

Other dog owners seek advice about solving the dog's aggression problem. Often this advice includes, "You have to be the Alpha Dog, and the way to become the top dog is to do the Alpha Roll."

What Does the Term "Alpha Dog" Mean?

"Alpha" is the first letter of the Greek alphabet and when we use the word regarding dogs, it means "the first" or "top dog." Other terms you may have heard are "pack leader" or "dominant dog." In dog society, there is no democracy like we have. Dogs don't believe, "All dogs are equal and we each have the same rights." Leadership is an important concept to your dog. If your dog is not sure about whether or not you are in charge, your dog may just naturally try to take over. A conflict arises when we as people want to be in charge and just haven't made it clear to our dog.

Dog trainers who want to avoid this idea of being in charge may talk about the dog and the owner as a team. This comparison can apply if we realize that that a team operates under at least two rules. The first is the structure of the activity they are doing and the second is that teams have guidance in the form of a coach or a manager. Two people, or a dog and person just hanging around together are not a team.

One reason we have a problem with getting our dogs to respect us and mind us is that (just as with our children) we are concerned about our dog not loving us anymore if we do start setting rules. The key to helping you solve your dog's behavior problem is to change your dog's position in your family.

For your happiness and the happiness of your dog, it is very important that both you and your dog know and agree on your positions in your family. There are different ways to do this and it has become quite popular to have you as a person try to convince your dog that you are in charge by having you act like a dog. While this sounds good, it overlooks the fact that we are not dogs.

My purpose is to alert you to the fact that you can be in charge by acting like a person rather than trying to act like a dog.

Do I Have to Act Like the Alpha Dog?

You may be feeling uncomfortable about the fact that you have a dog that is biting. Adding to your concern is the idea that you have heard that you are going to have to act like a dog to get your dog to stop biting you. You are probably thinking, "I don't know anything about dogs and now I am going to have to act like one." This is like having someone ask you to act like the President of Mars. First of all, you don't know anything about life on Mars or what the average Martian citizen does, and you have even less of an idea what it is like being the President of Mars.

You may be thinking, "My dog is biting me even when I am standing up and I know that my dog is aggressive with other dogs.

If I start getting down on my hands and knees and acting like another dog, my dog might be even more inclined to bite me."

What is the Alpha Roll?

The Alpha Roll is a technique that has you wrestle your dog over on his back and hold him down until he gives up. You may have seen dogs do this to each other and it seems to work for them. You may wonder, "If it works with two dogs, why doesn't it always work with a person and a dog?"

This technique is based on the assumption that once the dog is rolled over on its back, the dog will become submissive and give up.

One question has puzzled me. I can understand that once this technique appeared in dog training books, people would go along with it and recommend it to others. I certainly tried it once myself. The question I have is, "Why would anyone think of this in the first place?" I suspect that someone made the mistake of observing dog behavior and also watching people wrestling on television and then tried to combine the two ideas. Quite honestly, if dogs did watch and believe in wrestling as seen on television, our chance of having the Alpha Roll work for us would be much greater.

You may have watched wrestling on television and seen someone who is 583 pounds pinned to the mat for the count of three. He gives up and walks out of the ring defeated. He picks up his check and goes home. Some soreheads will jump back in the ring and hit their opponents or an unlucky referee on the head with a folding chair, but we know that this all comes under a set of rules that governs wrestling. You get pinned down and you lose.

What would happen if you were twelve years old and you were wrestling with your twin and your twin cheated? You pin your twin down, count "one, two, three" and then release your twin's arms only to have your conquered opponent punch you in the nose. You would yell, "Hey, that's against the rules, I pinned you down and you were supposed to give up."

Unfortunately, your twin wasn't operating under the same rules that you were. The same thing can happen with dogs. Some dogs don't always give up when they are pinned in a submissive position. When two dogs fight with each other and one rolls over into a submissive position, he does so because he knows that the other dog on top could continue attacking him, even to the point of killing him.

Like the professional wrestlers, the dogs are operating under a set of rules, but we must remember that the dog rules are very different from wrestling rules. Dogs don't always abide by professional wrestling rules. When we use a technique based on wrestling rules and our dog does not agree with the rules, we can get hurt. Not only are we making the mistake of thinking the dog isn't playing by our rules, we also don't know the real dog rules that the dog is using. It would be like be like bringing a fencing foil to a pistol duel.

When you hold your dog down on his back, you are in danger because if your dog doesn't give up, you have to get up and get away before the dog can jump up and continue the fight. It is not a position you want to find yourself in.

This technique can work with soft dogs, but if your dog is pushy, be careful, don't use the Alpha Roll or you might get hurt.

My first experience was demonstrating the Alpha Roll in front of twenty-seven dog owners in a class in 1981. I announced that there was a new supposedly "natural technique" for dealing with biters.

The person who told me about the Alpha Roll said that when the dog bites you, you roll the dog over on its back, you hold the dog down, stare the dog in the eye and the dog is supposed to do three things. First, the dog is supposed to look to the side to avoid your direct eye contact. Next, the dog should stop struggling and go limp. Finally, the dog should piddle submissively as a way of showing that you are in charge.

I tried it with a three-month-old puppy who had never heard of the technique, and as I soon discovered, didn't have the slightest inclination to submitting to me just because I had rolled her over on her back.

I told my class that I had heard of a new "natural correction" for dogs and asked if anyone had a dog that bit. One woman who had previously taken a dog through my class offered me the leash of her Chow Chow. I knelt down next to the dog and gently picked up one of her feet to pet it. This is a way of testing a dog to see if the dog is willing to accept you doing something to her.

She immediately bit me. I made a comment inviting my students to watch to see what would happen. I turned her over on her back and held her down. Instead of averting her glance, going limp, and piddling submissively, this pup just glared at me with a very angry look and I could feel all of the tension in her body as I waited for her to submit. After a few seconds, I thought I would let her go and see what would happen. As soon as I released her, her head shot forward and she bit me. I immediately pinned her down again. A faint doubt entered my mind as I held her at arm's length. Was this going to work? I began to say things just to avoid the obvious conclusion that this was not working at all. "She is starting to submit," I said as I released her and she bit me again. She had very sharp puppy teeth and my hands were hurting from the bites. I pinned her down again and began to think of one of the dumbest things that I could recall and that is watching people who go around catching cobras and twelve foot pythons by hand. I wondered if, like them, I would be featured on "The World's Dumbest People" show. I switched to the future (hopeful) tense and announced, "She will start submitting soon."

Each time I let her up, she bit me again. After the sixth bite, she peed on me and it was not submissively. If she could have talked she probably would have said, "You failed to see the two problems with this technique. The first and most obvious is that I am not giving up as you hoped and the second is that because I am not giving up, you have to jump up from your kneeling position and get away before I bite you. Now that I have bitten you six times, I am expressing my opinion of you in the same way I would mark a tree. You would be wise to figure out a way to retreat."

Finally, my brain turned on and I realized that she had won. I reached under her neck and held her by the collar behind her head and I got up and walked her over to her owner and thanked her. I dismissed my class and went out to my car to go to the hospital to get my hands treated. As I drove to the emergency room, I had two thoughts. The first was that this was the stupidest thing I had ever done in my life. The second was a feeling of relief that the dog had bitten me instead of a student. What would have happened if I had taught this technique to a student who tried it and got bitten in front of all of the other students? I am sure that an attorney attending this class would have seen a lawsuit unfolding as he watched me teach a technique in front of all the witnesses that resulted in the injury of a dog owner attempting the Alpha Roll.

I believe that my job as someone who teaches others how to work with their dogs involves teaching them things they can do effectively and as safely as possible.

After this experience, I have warned all of my students in my Week One classes not to attempt the Alpha Roll. At the end of one class, a man came up at the end of the first class and gruffly said, "I wish I came here first." I asked him what he meant and he showed me a ¾ inch scar on his nose where his four-month-old Rottweiler had bitten him. His veterinarian had showed him the technique. It worked when the veterinarian did it, but when he went home and tried it, his dog bit him on the nose. I was very lucky to have understood the part of the Alpha Roll that says you are supposed to look the dog in the eye to mean, "but don't get your face too close." This man had been told that you had to get your face close to the dog's face.

Veterinarians who recommend this have two advantages over the dog owner when they demonstrate this technique. First, the dog is up on a slippery examination table which lessens the dog's confidence. The second advantage the veterinarian has over the dog owner is a lot of confidence built on years of experience. Dogs sense this and display submissive behavior at the veterinarian's office, but then when the dog is back at home, the dog owner attempts the technique and the dog may not respond.

What's Wrong With the Alpha Roll?

As I looked at this experience, I analyzed what had gone wrong. Here are the problems with using this Alpha Roll technique, including how it can backfire and become dangerous. After each statement, there will be two points made. The first will have to do with your safety and the second will be about the training implications of what you are doing.

1. Your face is close to your dog's face.

The safety concern is that if your face is close to your dog's face, you are in greater danger of getting bitten on the face.

The training concern is that if your face is close, you increase the threat to your dog. That may be to your advantage if you can intimidate your dog, but if your stubborn dog isn't intimidated, he will resist even more. There is an expression, "I'm going to get in your face." It means that the person is going to be as confrontational as possible. Sometimes "in your face" works and sometimes it doesn't. If you were forced into having a fight with a person who could definitely beat you up, you might, as a last resort, step up to the person and try to bluff them by yelling directly in the person's face. What kind of feeling would you have if it did not work? You would think, "Well, I tried bluffing him and it didn't work. Now I am only inches away from someone who can pulverize me, what am I going to do?" You would have a feeling of impending doom.

Trying to confront and bluff a strong-willed dog in this manner makes little sense. When doing the Alpha Roll, you are close to you dog and if you are lacking confidence, your dog will sense your uncertainty.

The face-to-face position even when you are standing up is much more challenging than the side-by-side position. I have had good success working with biters and dogs that are aggressive toward other dogs because I keep them next to me, rather than being face to face with them.

2. You are on your hands and knees while doing this technique.

The safety concern is that it is difficult to get up and away from the dog if the dog does not give up. The time it takes us to get up off your hands and knees is greater than the time it takes the dog to roll up from its back and bite you.

The training concern is that by getting down on your hands and knees, you are giving up your dominant height advantage. I believe that one of the reasons dogs do respect us is that we are taller. I had a student in a class who was 6'2" and who had a Great Dane. When she first came in, she said she had reached down to pet her dog while he was lying down and he jumped her and tried biting her. She managed to stop him and wondered what could be done to prevent it from happening again. Because I have hard wood floors I never get down and interact with my dogs on the floor. I also don't find floors particularly comfortable even when they are carpeted so I don't spend any time on any floor. Apparently, this student would get down on the floor and play with her Great Dane. As soon as she said that, I suggested that she stay up off the floor because she was losing all of her height advantage with her dog. If your dog is friendly and you want to play on the floor with your dog, go ahead. If your dog is pushy or aggressive, don't get down to your dog's level.

Another disadvantage we have when we get down to the dog's level is that we have just two hands to protect our body. When the dog is on its back, it has four feet and a mouth full of teeth for you to contend with.

3. You may not be strong and physically fit enough to hold the dog down until the dog submits. You also may lack the determination, confidence, and ability to hold the dog down in the submissive position.

The safety concern is that you may let go or get tired and lose your grip and then have to let the dog go before the dog gives in. I saw one man hold a dog down for more than twenty-five minutes. As soon as he let the dog up, the dog tried to bite him. Holding onto anything for that long can be a challenge. Losing your grip or having to let go could give the dog a chance to bite you.

The training concern is that any time that you allow a dog to win, the dog is more likely to resist the next time. Your struggle with your dog also will escalate if your dog is allowed to come out on top. When dealing with an aggressive dog, one of two things will happen. You will succeed in getting the aggression under control or the dog will get worse.

Along with lacking the physical strength, determination, and courage to actually do the Alpha Roll, you may not even be able to quickly make the decision to do it. Your dog will detect your indecision. This might confuse your dog.

If it takes you too long to do this technique, the dog may not make the connection between the original misbehavior and the ultimate outcome of the Alpha Roll. The best training involves setting the dog up so that after the dog gets corrected for doing something wrong, the dog is immediately presented with the same temptation. This allows the dog to make a decision. Either do it right and get praised, or do it wrong again and get corrected again. This means that corrections should be fast and effective and easily repeated by the dog owner.

Your indecision also may invite a very confident dog to take advantage of you.

There is swiftness and decisiveness involved in the behavior of dogs that some of us find hard to imitate. Our lack of these characteristics can be glaringly obvious to the dog.

Do We Really Know How to Be Dogs?

Most of us are not good at being dogs. As people, we are better at some things and worse at other things. You are comfortable doing what you know how to do, just as I am comfortable teaching dog classes. If you were put in charge of doing something you knew nothing about, you would lose your confidence and the people who depended on you would know that you don't know what you are doing.

Yes, there does need to be a way of you showing your dog that you are in charge. We can best do this by maintaining our height advantage. Given the number of problems people have dealing with their own lives it seems a stretch to ask a person to become "top dog" in a convincing way.

Why Do We Use Ideas Like This?

I believe there are several reasons why these ideas appeal to us. The first is because we think that this is the way dogs act with each other. We think that dogs must know something we don't know. Thinking this prompts us to look at dogs and assume that they have all the answers and that we must copy their actions. This is akin to the idea that floated around when I went to college in the late 1960s, that we adults should go to the day care centers and watch children and learn how to be more childlike.

Having people act like the top dog may be an effort to help us stop treating dogs like people. When we treat dogs like people, we can be disappointed because dogs do not always live up to our elevated expectations.

Some of us have a problem accepting the fact that people and animals are not equal. This is not a matter of whether dogs are better or worse than people, merely an acceptance of the fact that we people have created a world that is not natural for the dog. Because we have traffic, property rights, and laws about what dogs can and cannot do, we have an obligation to teach dogs about our world rather than learning how to deal with them in their own natural world. Time has proven that dogs are better at adapting to us than we are trying to act like dogs.

In my twenty-four years experience as a dog trainer, I have been bitten six times in classes. One involved the Alpha Roll, three involved trying to get the dog to lie down, and the last two were when the dog tried biting its owner. The first four all included the same elements: my being face to face with the dog, my bending down (giving up my dominant position), and putting my hands near the dog's mouth. I have learned to maintain my height advantage with a pushy dog.

One Good Use for the Alpha Roll

The roll over technique can be used as a test for selecting a puppy. You can use it to determine the degree of stubbornness a puppy has. If the pup gives up easily it will be a submissive pup. If the pup fights you, you realize that it will much more assertive. You can use it as a test because it is not essential that the puppy learns anything from this test and you do not have to win.

Special Warning

Even if you have a submissive dog that readily allows you to roll him over on his back, be careful not to do this in front of your children. If your child watches you doing the Alpha Roll, your child may attempt it with the family dog. An even greater danger exists if your child tries to do it with a strange dog.

What Happens If You Try It in Public?

If your dog tries to bite you in public and you use the Alpha Roll, you may find others standing and watching you and asking, "What are you doing to the dog?" This involvement of others may distract you at a time when your total concentration is needed. While this may happen with other corrections used in training a dog not to bite, the nature of this technique and the amount of time it can take may invite comments and criticism from bystanders that will distract you while you are doing the Alpha Roll. The last thing you need when your dog is biting you is to have someone come over to you and start telling you that you are being mean to your dog.

Letter of Concern

In conclusion, I am going to share a letter that I sent to a friend of mine who trains dogs in another state.

Dear Friend:

We have a difference of opinion and I want to see if I can smooth it out. I'd like to clarify my position on the Alpha Roll. First, I believe that if you feel like it is the right thing to do for you personally, that is something I can accept with two reservations. I am concerned for your safety. I also am concerned about the potential liability that could injure both your reputation and injure you financially. You have worked very hard to build your reputation. As your friend, I am proud of you and what you have done and I do not want to see you being hurt either physically or financially.

You are in much better physical condition than your students are and you also possess a degree of determination that is very strong. I am sure that if anyone can get the Alpha Roll to work, you would be the one to do it.

I am concerned that having our students seeing either of us getting bitten would cause them to think, "Does my instructor know what is going on?" Even more important is the idea, "If my instructor gets bitten with his years of experience, how in the world am I as a new dog owner going to do it?"

I question the effectiveness of the technique. A correction should be a negative consequence. Is the Alpha Roll a negative consequence? I have come to the conclusion, "Not always."

The danger is that a hard-headed dog may consider it merely a momentary nuisance.

You may have been fortunate in having had better luck with this technique than I have. Perhaps you have not been bitten and perhaps none of your students have gotten bitten.

Training dogs involves risk and training protection dogs involves an even greater risk.

I believe that the reason a dog will roll over and submit to another dog is that the submissive dog knows that the tougher dog has the option of even more aggression. When we as people do it, it is as if we are able to accomplish nine steps out of a ten-step process. Lacking the tenth step, we find ourselves nearly succeeding and then having to repeat the process over and over.

In one brief conversation that we had on this subject, you mentioned that I may not need it in class, but with tougher protection dogs certain corrections may not be adequate. I agree with you 100 percent. More of your dogs need tougher corrections. Where we differ in opinion is that I don't feel that the Alpha Roll is tough enough because it doesn't work that well with the pushy dogs you work with.

I hope you understand my concern for you and for your students' safety.

Appendix E

Q & A

Q: *We are going to have a baby. Should we get a dog before or after the baby is born?*

A: If you are getting the dog just for your child, you should wait until your child is five or six years old. If you personally want a dog or you already have a dog, be sure to train it before the baby arrives.

Q: *Our child really wants to get a puppy. When is the best time?*

A: Puppies have an almost universal appeal to children. We at one time had four dogs and three cats but that didn't stop one of the kids from asking, "Can we get a puppy?"

I cannot keep track of how many moms have called me and said, "Our child wanted a puppy and promised to take care of it and now I have to do it all."

I think that the smart thing to do is to test your child's developmental ability and emotional commitment to care for a dog with something like a goldfish or a hamster. If the thrill wears off in a week and they don't take care of it, you will know.

On the other hand, if you as an adult in a family want the dog and realize and willingly accept that you will be taking care of the dog, get it.

Q: *Can I get my dog to mind my family?*

A: Some classes have a one dog, one owner rule. I encourage you to bring your family members to a class. If your primary goal is to turn out a well-trained dog to perform in a television commercial, then one person will be best. But, your real goal should be to have your family and dog live happily together.

You do need to keep in mind two important points. The first is that most dogs don't consider young children under eight years old to be people, but more like siblings. What this means to you is that while some younger children may seem to do well with your dog, you should never leave a young child alone with a dog. Nor should you expect a young child to supervise a dog.

The second point is that, unfortunately, dogs are smart enough to know which family members will make them mind. I believe that children are also smart enough to know the same thing.

Some people want to know if I will take their dog and train it for them. I never do this because week after week, I work with dogs in class and then hand them back to their owners and if the owner doesn't do what I do, the dog will misbehave. The dog will not automatically transfer its training from me to its owner. I tell people, "I won't take your dog and train him, but I will take you the owner in for training and teach you how to be effective with your dog."

Q: *What is the right age to get a puppy and when should training begin?*

A: Getting a puppy at seven to eight weeks is ideal. If you get a puppy over three months, be sure the pup has been socialized properly. If your pup shows signs of shyness, go to the nearest supermarket. Sit outside the store with your puppy and have hundreds of people visit with the pup.

I let pups start training any time after seven weeks of age. Some veterinarians insist on you waiting until four months when the pups have completed the puppy vaccinations. I let people start earlier because some pups can be so difficult that people get rid of them before four months. Two- to five-month-old pups can learn, although I don't expect reliability from them. After five months, I expect dogs to be able to keep up with the older dogs in a regular training class and schedule.

Seven to ten months is the teenage time for dog. They are likely to test the limits at this stage. It would be wise to get in for training before this time.

Q: *What about getting an older dog?*

A: "Free to good home" is a popular expression. When I see that I assume a family is having a problem with a dog and they want to get rid of it. The problem they have may not matter to you and you certainly can find good older dogs out of the newspaper or at your animal shelter. The advantage of getting an older dog is that, along with skipping over the young puppy issues, you have a pretty good idea of what the dog is like. Older dogs can be trained. But, when dogs lose their hearing and their vision, it is hard to train them.

When you get an older dog, train the dog. Don't expect that just because the dog is older, he will be perfect for you. People do have to get rid of great dogs, but when I get an older dog, I realize that he may not have met the first owner's expectations. In other words, if the dog is perfect, why are they giving him away?

Q: *When do you start training?*

A: I start the day I get the puppy or dog. Some have the idea, "We will let him get used to us for a month and then train the dog." If I was a child and you adopted me, you wouldn't let me hang around the house for a month to get used to you before you showed me how to live with you. Training is teaching the dog how to get used to you. Start as soon as you can. Training and parenting are not things that you do for five or twenty minutes at a time and then ignore the principles the rest of the day. They are showing your dog and your child how to live. Use every chance you can to train your dog and teach your child.

Q: *Should you get a mixed breed or a purebred dog?*

A: The good thing about getting a purebred dog is predictability. The bad thing is that you may not want what you should have known you were getting. One man called and said his dog was terrible about pulling. When I asked him what breed he had, he told me, "Alaskan Malamute." Another person called and said that she wanted to start my class but they decided to get rid of their dog because he got too big. She had gotten a St. Bernard. There is information about the purebred dogs that might alert a prospective dog owner that sled dogs pull and the St. Bernard breed gets big.

Be familiar with the breed characteristics of your dog. Knowing what a dog was bred to do can help you select the right dog.

If a dog was bred for chasing, fighting, or aggressive behavior, be careful that you know this ahead of time. If your dog was bred to do things away from you like hunt by sight or scent, you might pay extra attention to training your dog not to run away.

Other breed characteristics like wanting to be in water, carrying things, pulling, digging, barking, and high activity levels may help you be prepared for behaviors that may turn into problems.

Q: *Where should I go for advice?*

A: If your car broke down, you would not go to your accountant any more than you would take your tax questions about your automobile to your auto mechanic. Notice that while both deal with an aspect of automobile usage, they may not know anything about other aspects of automobile usage. The same is true of people involved with dogs, including breeders, groomers, veterinarians, and trainers. I do not give advice on breeding, grooming, or veterinary care because I am not an expert in breeding, grooming, or veterinary care. Be sure that you ask experts questions only in their field of expertise.

Q: *Can I trust my breeder for training advice?*

A: You can learn about dogs from breeders. Be aware that breeders love their breed. When I talk to breeders I always think of the bumper sticker that says, "Ask me about my grandchildren." I don't think anyone has ever actually responded to that bumper sticker, but if you did, you would expect to get a glowing account of the wonderful grandchild. Breeders know a lot about the history of their breed and what the dogs should look like, but they don't always know a lot about training. Understand that while breeders show their dogs at dog shows, many of them think obedience training ruins the dog for the show ring. If you went to a dog show with two thousand dogs and asked all of the breeders if they would trust any of their dogs to mind off-leash, at least nineteen hundred would say no and look at you like you were a fool for even asking. Getting accurate training advice from some breeders can be difficult.

Some breeders have the idea that all of the other breeds in the world benefit from training, but not theirs. "Our breed is different," is their motto. While dogs certainly have been bred for different purposes and many do have specific natural abilities, they still benefit from training.

In one of the strangest situations I ever encountered, a family with a very large, powerful dog called me for help because the dog had bitten two of their children. I had the hardest time convincing them that their dog should go to a training class. They finally brought the dog in and when I asked them what was their reason for hesitating, they said that the breeder told them that the dog had natural abilities and didn't need training. This was a half-truth in that the dog did have very strong, natural abilities as a guard dog, but did need training so the dog would stop protecting the parents from the children.

Q: *How should I start choosing a breed?*

A: Recognize your strengths and weaknesses. There are several things that I am very good at. There are other things I am not good at. After crashing my friend's snowmobile into a tree and paying $1,200 to have it repaired, I avoid machines with handlebars and motors. I find my life is happiest when I do what I am good at and avoid doing things that hurt me or cost me money.

If you have a very strong personality, you might do well with a breed that is always testing the limits. On the other hand, if you are mild-mannered, the pushy dog will drive you crazy. When people call and ask me about getting a breed that I know is pushy, I diplomatically ask how they do with making their children mind them. If they have trouble setting up rules for their kids and sticking with them, a mild-mannered breed will be a better choice.

Index

About the Author

Harold R. Hansen has a master's degree from the University of Oregon and taught at Thurston High School for two years. He opened "Heeling Free" Dog School in 1976 and has helped thousands of people with their dogs' behavior problems. He has never turned a dog down for training and has worked with biters, as well as dogs that have killed sheep, chickens, dogs, and cats.

At fifty-one, he became a stepdad. Growing up without a dad (who died when Harold was one year old), Harold created this parenting guide to help himself.

He also has written a puppy booklet, a student handbook for his dog training class, and a SCUBA diver's guide.

He and his family live in Eugene, Oregon.